After Winter Comes the Summer

Lorraine Anson (in green) and Sheryll Titford in the Pūhoi hall in 2016 celebrating the anniversary of the arrival of the *Liverpool* in Auckland and the third wave of 31 Bohemian settlers in March 1866.
Christine Krippner

After Winter Comes the Summer

Pūhoi's musical heritage in song, rhyme and dance

Roger Buckton, Ralf Heimrath and Judith Williams

MASSEY UNIVERSITY PRESS

In memory of Judith Williams QSM
30 January 1946–28 November 2022

Contents

Puhoi Choir singing *Egerlander Volkssingmesses* (by Franz Roscher, arranged by Peter Cammell) in the Church of Saints Peter and Paul in 2016. Judith Williams is standing fifth from left, Jenny Schollum eighth from left and at right in pink is the director of the children's choir Carole Hay, with musical director Alan Wagstaff behind. *PHS 3390a*

A message from the German Ambassador to New Zealand

German-language dialects are a vital part of the language as a whole and reflect the movement and history of German-speaking peoples over thousands of years. Pūhoi, New Zealand, is one of the farthest-flung outposts to be home to a unique dialect.

The material in this book has been collected at the latest possible point in time — starting 100 years after settlement, when songs were still recalled and sung by maturing grandchildren of the pioneering settlers. For a hundred years they were part of a musical life wherever the German-Bohemians lived, but at the time of emigration in 1863 many of these songs already possessed a heritage of centuries in European village society. These are not songs from a court and upper-class milieu which may well have been published, but simply, dialect songs that have been passed from generation to generation and settled in that once far-away country of New Zealand.

I am grateful that the three authors have devoted their time and expertise to put together and annotate this collection. The publication of the songs means they can be enjoyed for many years to come: a reminder of a unique cultural heritage.

I wish you much joy in singing these wonderful songs.

Nicole Menzenbach
German Ambassador to New Zealand
Wellington 2025

Foreword

In 1863 a small band of 83 adults and children travelled from Bohemia, in a region now part of the Czech Republic, to arrive in Pūhoi, 50 miles north of Auckland. They carried with them memories of family and singing in their homes and villages. In the subsequent years, others followed them. They brought with them the violin, the dudelsack (a type of bagpipe from Bohemia) and the accordion, traditional musical instruments from their homeland.

Songs and dances kept the Pūhoi settlers going as they struggled to develop their allocated land. Their language — a German dialect — formed a bond that also kept them together. Education and integration with other settlers would ease the Bohemians' isolation. So English became the mode of communication for them and for the related Bohemian settlement of Ōhaupō.

When I attended the 1963 centennial celebrations (as a descendant), third-generation Bohemians still remembered some of the old songs and dances. Families who were strong in music had formed a band which regularly brought folk together for dancing. The celebration marked this heritage with dancing and singing — it remains my most precious memory.

Some 10 years of research brought this book to fruition. It is a marvellous treasure of an early settlement's importance to New Zealand's music history. Many of the songs had fortunately been recorded or written in notebooks over several decades. Bringing together research on the music, the language and the associated stories has been a collective's work, including those with academic skills and work by dedicated local people.

Pūhoi's musical heritage is a taonga for New Zealand. It provides people and students of history with ways of enjoying the past in the present. Each year the anniversary of the settlement is celebrated on 29 June with dancing and warm hospitality. The date is also significant as the Feast of Saints Peter and Paul, the name given to the local church in thanksgiving for the migration.

High school students, forced during Covid years to work at home, broke their isolation by adopting their traditional dancing. For them and other students, this book offers an entry into their history as well as recent experience. A small museum at Pūhoi holds many of these stories and presents fragments of early history to locals and visitors, and 29 June remains a special day for marking Pūhoi's past. This book tempts all to venture off the highway to enjoy this special place.

Dame Claudia Orange
Historian and Pūhoi descendant
Auckland 2025

PART ONE

Pūhoi's songs and rhymes

Judith Williams' study, with her house behind, at Pūhoi in 2019. The study was the venue for many meetings about the songs in this book. Both the study and the house were demolished following the catastrophic flood in Pūhoi on 27 January 2023. *Roger Buckton*

1.
The sources

The embryo for this song collection is to be found in the notebooks of Judith Williams, a long-time resident of Pūhoi who majored in German language at university and used this knowledge as a basis for later personal studies in Deitsch — the vernacular language of the older Bohemians (referred to locally as the 'dialect'). In her notebooks we can find common phrases, local ditties and relevant and interesting vocabulary which she had informally collected in the 1960 and 1970s from the few dozen Bohemians who could still speak Deitsch. To assist English speakers with pronunciation in the Puhoian accent, she contrived her own spellings, taking care to distinguish the Pūhoi dialect from High German.

Of special interest were the songs that people remembered, for it was evident that there was a common core of songs recalled by those Williams interviewed. Phonetically this had the advantage that varying pronunciations of the same phrases could be noted and lapses in memory by one respondent might be remedied by another. The notebooks have to be seen in light of Williams's own purpose in recording the songs: to teach herself Deitsch. As such, she did not record her respondents on audiotape, nor did she attempt to notate in music the songs that they sang. Her records provide only the text.

As a song collection, much of Judith's work is based on the significant fieldwork of Werner Otto Droescher (1911–1978), who specialised in linguistics at the German Department of the University of Auckland. Like Williams, his interests centred on the linguistic aspects of the language rather than the music per se. In transcribing the texts of the songs, he was inclined to spell the dialect in terms of High German. However, Droescher's major contribution was that he used a tape recorder and recorded all his research interviews. The more than 12 hours of reel-to-reel recordings of interviews were later copied onto compact discs (CDs) and housed at the Manuscripts and Archives collection of the University of Auckland.

In addition to personal interviews, Droescher recorded community singing in the Pūhoi hall as part of the 1963 centennial celebrations. This remarkable recording provides evidence of a community of ageing Bohemians who knew and could still sing some of the most-loved dialect songs.

In 1976 Radio New Zealand, as part of the *Spectrum* documentary series, visited the Pūhoi pub and discussed old times with four of the male patrons. They sang *Gsundhait mainer und Gsundhait dainer* to broadcaster Jack Perkins and this is available as an RNZ podcast.

The last-known person in New Zealand who could speak the dialect was Frederick (Fred) Rauner (1928–2022). In 2017 he was living in Orewa, on the coast just south of Pūhoi, and was an accordionist in the Puhoi Band alongside his brother Laurie. In a recorded interview with Judith Williams and Roger Buckton, Rauner discussed and sang the songs that he recalled.

In a similar vein, songs and fragments were obtained from the internet site of Gerard Straka, who had recorded his father Ben singing the songs during the 1980s. Other songs were sung by Annie Rauner (1901–1999) and recorded on cassette recorder by her niece Dorothy Berger, who gave them to Roger Buckton in 1993.

The transcriptions of music and text from these various sound recordings, used in combination with Williams's language notebooks, provide the basis for most of the songs in this collection.

Droescher identified the Pūhoi dialect as North Bavarian, originating from the region of Staab in southern Egerland.[1] This dialect, which has virtually disappeared in Pūhoi, is still known in Germany. This has resulted in the published music collections of Erich Baumann being another important source in reproducing

Top row, left to right: Charles Becher, 1901. *PHS 0686;* Annie Rauner (née Bayer) c. 1940s. *PHS 0673;* Werner Droescher, 1946. *Werner Otto Droescher papers. 1962–1978. MSS & Archives A-199, folder 1. Special Collections, University of Auckland Libraries and Learning Services/Herbert Tornquist*

Middle row, left to right: Erich Baumann, 1984. *PHS 4278a;* Fred Rauner, 2019. *Roger Buckton*

Below: The cover of the original Puhoi Band audio cassette (1993), featuring Fred Rauner, Philip Wech, Ben Bayer, Dot Berger and Laurie Rauner. *Recorder Centre*

the songs. *Alt-Egerländer Tänze* (1985) and *Egerländer Volkslieder* (1990) contain several songs and pieces which Baumann collected from Pūhoi residents Laurie Rauner, Ben Straka and Anton Bayer during a visit in 1984.

There are other publications of folk music from Germany that have been useful in learning more about a particular song and these are noted on the individual song's page and in the appendix, Song origins and text variations, supported by the bibliography. The most important of these is Albert Brosch's *Der Liederschatz des Egerlandes* (1986), see p. 65.

While the words are the focus of a song, the music has more than just a supporting role. This is even more true as the language fades and song texts are forgotten. Then it is the melodies that carry on, as they have done through the traditional instruments of Pūhoi's music — the accordion, violin and dudelsack (Bohemian bagpipe). An important instrumental source is the manuscript book of Charles Becher (1874–1956), one of the few musicians in the early years who could read music.

Two CDs — *The Puhoi Band* and *The Accordions of Puhoi* — were recorded in 1993 and 1996 respectively by Roger Buckton. In compiling the repertoire for the CDs, Laurie Rauner, assisted by Ben Bayer, was asked to include only their old Bohemian songs. Rauner said that the tunes came from the old songs but that the song texts had been lost over the years. Thus the 50 pieces on the two CDs were complete tunes which had the potential to provide the musical glue for bonding fragments of song texts distilled from distant memories.

Werner Droescher at Wood Bay, Auckland, c. 1970. *Werner Otto Droescher papers. 1962–1978. MSS & Archives A-199, folder 1. Special Collections, University of Auckland Libraries and Learning Services.*

Werner Droescher

Werner Droescher's field recordings have provided most of the raw data for many of these songs as transcribed by the authors. His success in establishing genuine and friendly relationships with his Bohemian informants can be attributed to his life-views and extraordinary experiences in Germany, Spain, New Zealand and Australia.

Born in Mannheim, Germany in 1911, Droescher attended an alternative teachers' training academy in Altona, Hamburg in 1930 and 1931. At this time, he realised that Nazi ideology was beginning to assert itself, and at a rally organised by Goebbels he sensed that a 'mass hysteria' was taking place. He made the decision to leave Germany and secured a position in Tossa, Catalonia, Spain, as a tutor for the son of a German hotelier.

There, he met English society belle Margaret Greville Foster (better known by her pen name Greville Texidor). The Spanish Civil War was looming and with similar anti-fascist views they both supported the Republican movement. By

1937 they were disillusioned with Europe and the prospect of a general war, and became interested in emigrating to New Zealand. With a view to facilitating this move, they married, but with war looming Droescher, as a German with apparent anarchist and communist sympathies, was interned in Devon (at a Butlins Holiday Camp commandeered by the government) while Greville was sent to Holloway Prison as a suspected anarchist with communist sympathies and the wife of a German national.

Happily, pressure from influential friends secured their release, but it was clear that they should leave England. And so, in 1940, with their daughter Cristina, they took the ship *Rangitata* to the port of Auckland.

After two unsettled months, Droescher welcomed the offer of a permanent job plus cottage with an elderly Quaker farmer, Josiah Homes, who lived at the remote settlement of Paparoa on the Kaipara Harbour, north of Auckland.

Paparoa (and Rawene, further up the west coast) was home to a number of people with 'alternative' life-style views, including Josiah Homes, and Werner settled quite comfortably into the demands of rural life. With time on her hands, Greville took up writing and befriended the influential author Frank Sargeson, and his circle of friends. After two years, they moved to a house on Auckland's North Shore and closer to Sargeson's bach in Takapuna. Their house became a popular place for writers, artists and intellectuals and Greville established a place as a successful author of novels and short stories.

Restless by nature, in 1948 Greville persuaded the family to move to Queensland, and later to New South Wales. There followed moves to Europe but Droescher struggled to find a permanent university position. In 1960 he successfully applied for a lectureship at the newly established German Department at the University of Auckland. Greville did not come with him, and three years later he was in Pūhoi recording these songs.

Based on *All the Juicy Pastures: Greville Texidor and New Zealand* by Margot Schwass (Wellington: Te Herenga Waka University Press, 2019).

2. Aotearoa New Zealand's songs in Deitsch

In 1819 the Habsburg Government in Vienna issued an order to collect and record folk music, songs and dances from the Austrian lands, which at that time included Bohemia, Moravia and Silesia.[2] About a hundred years later, Albert Brosch[3] collected over 2000 songs, children's dances, rhymes, ditties and games from the German-speaking Bohemians in a relatively small part of these lands known as the region of Egerland.[4]

That the government in Vienna in 1819 felt that it was important to collect and record this music demonstrates the significance attached to this taonga. The number of songs Brosch collected is an indication of the abundance and popularity of singing and dancing in these communities. In the absence of recorded sound, their only music was what they made themselves.

So in 1863, when a small band of 83 adults and children made their way from a region on the outskirts of the Egerland, near Pilsen, to a remote spot on the other side of the globe, they took with them their fond memories of family and village singing and dancing. In the following years, their traditional musical instruments arrived — the violin, accordion and dudelsack (Bohemian bagpipe).

As the Egerlanders settled in and around Pūhoi, 80 kilometres north of Auckland, their songs and dances kept them going through hard times in a land

A postcard showing Bohemian dancing around the 1890s. Could it have reflected a similar evening in Pūhoi? Note the musicians at the top left with fiddle, clarinet and dudelsack. *Michael Cwach Collection*

in which they were isolated geographically and linguistically. These songs had been sung and enjoyed in Europe for hundreds of years and they survived an epic voyage lasting 106 days from London to Auckland. They were then sung by three generations of Bohemians in an isolated settlement in the north of New Zealand at a time when English was fast becoming the dominant language.

Fifty years later, the *New Zealand Herald* reported that 'the people were exceedingly fond of dancing, and maintained the quaint Bohemian dances . . . Perched up in one corner, on a couple of boxes, would be the bagpiper, with his dudelsac[k], and the fiddler . . .'[5]

During the following decades, the English language usurped Deitsch and the Bohemians integrated with the surrounding local people of mainly British descent. Despite this, in 1963, at the time of the centennial celebrations of the Bohemians' arrival in Pūhoi, there were enough third-generation Bohemians to remember about 20 of the original songs. Fortunately, many of these were captured on tape recorder or written down in notebooks. The songs, rhymes and stories that follow are the result of 10 years of research. They are the few songs that have survived along with their words. Happily, there are also many other tunes, without text, that continue to be played to this day.

We cannot know why this handful of folksongs survived from the many hundreds that were sung by the original Bohemians in both Pūhoi and Ōhaupō (near Hamilton), and perhaps further afield. Their texts and tunes inform us about the settlers from the other side of the world and, though greatly reduced in number, the remaining few are all the more valuable because they did survive. They are now New Zealand's taonga and, as such, are presented here for all New Zealanders to appreciate and enjoy.

In her 1934 thesis on the history of Pūhoi, Ruth Schmidt noted: 'country peasants gathered from rural towns and villages . . . they represented many grades of society, from the landless labourer to large landowner . . . among the working people were foresters, farm-labourers, miners, shepherds, cow-herds, domestic servants and dairy maids.'

A glance at the texts of these songs tells us that these Bohemian settlers were a rural people concerned with country issues. Animals, crops and the weather were all-important, as were feelings and relationships (especially those that led to marriage) and concerns about social status. They entertained and educated their children through song and music, and most had a mischievous sense of humour. They definitely enjoyed a drink or two and, of course, they loved to dance.

Salzmann and Scheufler describe a procession during the carnival season of Fasching:

> The procession included several masked figures — usually a bear, an old woman carrying a basket on her back with an old man in it, a Jew, and several 'runners'. . . . Humorous masked figures who ran around the edges of the procession keeping the group in order . . . People danced through the night on Sunday, again Monday evening until morning, and on Tuesday evening until midnight.[6]

A similar enthusiasm and endurance for dancing continued to be shown by the settlers in Pūhoi:

> All their great festivals are celebrated generally by a great three or four days' dance. On these occasions you see them drop on the floor from exhaustion.

One old man was pointed out to me who is at the very least sixty years, and whose passion for dancing is so great that once he is fairly started, no amount of entreaty will induce him to desist. Dance he will, without food or sleep, until his friends, taking compassion on his exhausted condition, seize him and nail his wooden shoes to the floor . . .[7]

Chotieschau (Czech: Chotěšov) was the home town of many of Pūhoi's Bohemian settlers. A detail of this painting by Gustav Zindel (1883–1959) depicts a procession during the carnival season (Fasching in German and Masopust in Czech), a three-day period that culminated on the Tuesday before Ash Wednesday (that is, 46 days before Easter) and signalled the beginning of Shrovetide. Notice the musicians with the clarinet, violin and dudelsack (the same as shown on p. 20) and the yellow trousers and blue coats of the men, typical of Chotieschau costumes (Die Tracht). These same colours can be seen at the celebrations for the 150th anniversary of settlement at Ōhaupō on p. 109. *Muzeum Karlovy Vary*

Ships that brought Bohemians to Aotearoa New Zealand, 1860–1876

Lord Burleigh

Departed London 18 November 1859. Arrived Auckland 22 March 1860. 14 Bohemians. Captain Martin Krippner and Mrs Emily Krippner and family, future couple Hans Krippner and Elizabeth Turnwald, and the Pankratz and Scheidler families.

War Spirit

Departed London 12 March 1863. Arrived Auckland 27 June 1863. 84 Bohemians. Families: Glatz, Karl, Michael Krippner, Pittner, Rauch, Martin Schischka, John Schollum, Lorenz Turnwald, Becher, Jesensky, Kaes, Paul, Podlesak, Rauner, Russek, Anton Turnwald. Singles: Bayer, Dobner, Remiger, Schober, Fitzthum, Krohn, Reisima, Soukup, Schuster, Straka, Tolhopf and Vlach.

Liverpool

Departed London 8 November 1865. Arrived Auckland 5 March 1866. 31 Bohemians. Families: Plescher, Lorenz Schischka, John Wech, Joseph Wech, John Wenzlick, future couple Maria Schott and Gregor Wenzlick. Singles: Anna and Maria Wenzlick.

Queen Bee

Departed London 20 July 1872. Arrived Auckland 29 October 1872. 15 Bohemians. Families: Anton Schischka, Schollum brothers, future couple Adalbert Wenzlick and Maria Fischer. Singles: Bayer, Heidler, Stiller, Turnwald and Wenzlick.

Friedeburg

Departed Hamburg 10 May 1875. Arrived Napier 24 August 1875. 12 Bohemians. Families: Hendl and Gruber. Singles: Fritsch, Remiger, Gauga and Wech.

A sketch of *Lord Burleigh* entering the Rangitoto channel, Auckland, in 1860 by E. H. Snow. *Werner Otto Droescher papers. 1962–1978. MSS & Archives A-147, folder 1b. Special Collections, University of Auckland Libraries and Learning Services*

Shakespeare

Departed Hamburg 7 October 1875. Arrived Wellington 23 January 1876.

29 Bohemians. Families: Multrus, Paul, Platz, Schedewy, Wenzl, Schiochka and Sittauer.

Terpsichore

Departed London 15 November 1875. Arrived Wellington 15 March 1876.

9 Bohemians. Families: Jedlitschka and Papesch.

Information supplied by Jenny Schollum, Puhoi Heritage Museum

3.
Index of the music and rhymes

Songs

Music for dancing

Rhymes

4.
Songs about the seasons and animals

Nao an Winta kinnt da Summa

After winter comes the summer

Medley: Summer air in May waltz

Literal translations from Deitsch

English	*High German*
After the winter, the summer comes, but it doesn't thunder, etc.	Nach dem Winter kommt der Sommer, aber donnern tut es nicht, etc.

Fred Rauner provided another text which can be used as a second verse if required:

In heaven, there is lightning, and thundering too, etc.
In Himm'l, dout's Gwittern un Donnern dout's aa, etc

Notes

This comical song was recorded on audio cassette by Dorothy Berger and given to Roger Buckton in 1993. The cassette recording provides two renditions of *Nao an Winta kinnt da Summa* by Berger's aunt, Annie Rauner. The repetitive nature of her words suggests that she may have forgotten some, and she only sang *lah, lah, lah* for the opening phrase of *In d'Stod eifoahrn* (p. 70). Happily, the melodic line of *Nao an Winta kinnt da Summa, In d'Stod eifoahrn* and *A Räuscherl im Kopf* (p. 86) is notated as a waltz medley entitled *Summer air in May* in Charles Becher's manuscript book. There are two variants of *In d'Stod eifoahrn* and these are bars 11–21 and bars 22–36. In this way, three known songs in Deitsch have been joined to make a medley of tunes suitable for dancing the waltz. In a situation where the original language is being forgotten, these melodies now provide another function — music for dancing.

The song is an example of a *Gstanzl* or *Schnadahüpfl.* Typically, these are humorous, often satirical, pub songs of four lines where one singer sings an opening line and another singer invents a new stanza in reply. If these improvised stanzas are appreciated, they are remembered and spread as new versions of the old song. The words are thus constantly changing.

In performance, the entire medley could be played as an instrumental, as is usually the case in Pūhoi. Alternatively, it could be performed in the European fashion in which *Nao an Winta* is sung and then the rest becomes an instrumental interlude, with or without dancing.

SOURCES *Text and music:* Recording of Annie Rauner (née Bayer) collected by Dorothy Berger and transcribed by Roger Buckton. *Music manuscript:* Charles Becher manuscript book. See also p. 146.

O du schäine Summablouma

O you pretty summer flower

Medley: Schedewy polka

Literal translations from Deitsch

English

O you pretty summer flower,
You've taken away my joy.
You are lying on my footstool
like an ox in the pigsty pool.

High German

O du schöne Sommerblume,
hast du mir meine Freude genommen.
Liegst du mir im Schemel drin
wie der Ochse im Saustall drin.

Notes

O du schäine Summablouma was collected by Judith Williams in the 1970s from Annie Rauner, Christina Wech and Bob Wech. In addition, Werner Droescher included it in his records collected in the 1960s. Music notation was not part of this data. However, it is notated in the Becher manuscript book as the first tune in a medley entitled *Schedewy polka.*

The *Schedewy polka* is a remarkable compilation of four songs: *O du schäine Summablouma, Baua heng dai(n) Bumml uu(n), Håns güih Huom* and *Wenn hält ma(n) Mutta.* Although the texts of many songs may be forgotten, they live on through their melodies being used in medleys and played at local dances. (The original text for this song is anti-Semitic in the final phrase and so another was substituted by the editors.)

The text of *O du schäine Summablouma* can be regarded as a priamel within the late medieval German tradition (a poem with four verses and double rhymes). This style of verse was first used on carnival stages and often culminated in a witty turn of phrase or interesting thought. A popular poet in this genre was Hans Rosenplüt (c. 1400–1460). As carnival events declined, the humour of this joking style of poetry was adopted by folksong. In southwest Germany, there is a similar verse, which was noted by Ernst Meier in his 1855 book *Schwäbische Volkslieder mit ausgewählten Melodien.*

O du schöne Sonnenblume,	O you pretty sunflower,
du hast mir mei Herz genumme,	you've taken my heart,
du liegst mir in meiner Haut,	you are lying in my skin,
wie die Worscht im Sauerkraut.	like the sausage in the sauerkraut (cabbage).

It was common practice to name pieces of music after local people and places, for example the *Schedewy polka* or *Waiwera waltz.* The Schedewy family were well known for their transport business, from the pioneering days when they moved huge kauri logs by bullock team to recent times running a trucking company.

SOURCES *Informants:* Annie Rauner, Christina Wech and Bob Wech, Judith Williams collection, also the informants for Werner Droescher in 1963. *Music:* Charles Becher manuscript book; Karl Euling (1977); Ernst Meier (1855). See also p. 147.

| Stalwart of the Pūhoi community Kelvin Schedewy in the early 1990s. *Mahurangi Matters*

D'Käi håm sua Spaß in Ham,
Däs is aa schwarz an glaam.

Cows have such fun in ponds,
That it is hard to believe.

Stephen and Eva Straka

Stephen and Eva Straka enjoy traditional kuchen made from cheese curd in their home at Pūhoi in the early 1990s. © *Arno Gasteiger*

Baua heng dai(n) Bumml ua(n)

Farmer, tie up your little bull

Literal translation from Deitsch

English	*High German*
Farmer, tie up your bull/little bull,	Bauer, häng dein' Bummel an,
so that he can't butt me.	dass er mich nicht stoßen kann.
If he butts me, I'll punish you.	Stößt er mich, so straf' ich dich.
A hundred dollars it'll cost you.	Hundert Dollar kost' er dich.
A hundred dollars is a lot of money,	Hundert Dollar ist ein Geld,
believe me, what I would like is	da glaub' mir einer, was mir g'fällt,
that he [the bull] plucks and picks me	dass [er] mich rupft und dass [er] mich zupft
and hops into bed with me.	und dass [er] mit mir ins Bett hinein hüpft.

Notes

The text and melody have been transcribed from the Droescher (1963) recording but the tune is the same as used in *Schedewy polka* (p. 30). The *Schedewy polka* was

John Rauner (1871–1958) in 1930 with his team of bullocks, used for pulling huge kauri logs and sometimes houses. *PHS 0263*

recorded by the Puhoi Band in 1993 and can also be found in the Charles Becher manuscript book. Several text and verse variations were collected from Alice Bayer and Tony Bayer by Judith Williams. The tune *Prince of Wales Schottischer* has also been used with this text.

The term 'dollar' means 'taler', which was an important silver coin in Europe, especially in the Austrian Empire and in Germany (taler is the origin of the word dollar).

The roots of this song can be found throughout most of the German-speaking areas of Europe including some linguistically isolated regions (language islands) which had been settled by Germans in earlier times.

SOURCES *Text and music:* Recording by Droescher (1963), transcribed by Ralf Heimrath and Roger Buckton. *Music manuscript:* Charles Becher manuscript book. *Informants:* Alice and Anton Bayer, Judith Williams collection. See also pp. 147–8.

Gickerl, wennst du niat krahst

Rooster, if you don't crow

Literal translation from Deitsch

English

Rooster, if you don't crow,
I'll turn your neck around.
Rooster, if you don't crow, [I'll] turn it around.
Turn it once, turn it twice, I'll turn it twice,
Turn it once, turn it twice, I'll turn it twice.

High German

Gockel, wenn du nicht krähst,
Dreh ich dein' Kragen um.
Gockel, wenn du nicht krähst, dreh ich ihn um.
Dreh ich ihn einmal um, dreh ich ihn zweimal um,
Dreh ich ihn einmal um, dreh ich ihn zweimal um.

Notes

Gickerl has an interesting pedigree. The melody is from a 1909 Edison phonograph recording. The Czech text on the same recording is:

Já si tě nevezmu, tys túze vospalá.	I won't take you, you are very sleepy,
Já si tě nevezmu, ty túze spíš.	I won't take you, you sleep too much.
Já jsem k tobě přišel, tys ještě ležela,	When I visited you, you were still in bed,
dal jsem ti hubičku, ty nic neviš.	I gave you a kiss, you didn't even notice.

An instrumental version of this song, entitled *Umandum,* may be heard on the CD *The Accordions of Puhoi.* It is one of the old Pūhoi circle dances. How did this Czech melody get to Pūhoi? It could have been brought from Europe as an instrumental piece for dancing, or as a song with the words in either Deitsch or Czech (although Czech was not used as a spoken language in Pūhoi, it is possible that some people knew the Czech words). Another possibility is that the Czech-speaking Chods — the ethnic neighbours of the Egerlanders — took the tune and made their own text.

While the Pūhoi settlers were a German-speaking community, they had lived in a region with a Czech-speaking population. A 1921 census in Chotieschau showed that there were 2089 German speakers and 681 Czech speakers. In the Egerland region as a whole, the German-speaking people were in the majority but the proportionate numbers for each village or town was variable. The Czech names of some of the settlers, for example Straka and Schischka, indicate that there were inter-cultural marriages.

In singing, the use of the same tune but with different words and meanings for each language suggest a genuine friendship between the two ethnicities, unaffected by the political aggression of the 20th century. Apart from this song, other tunes which are known in Czech include *O du schäine Summablouma, Eins und zwei und drei and vier* and *Finger polka.*

SOURCES *Text in Deitsch:* Ralf Heimrath. *Text in Czech: Dudy a dudácká muzika* (1909), The Oldest Recordings of Czech Folk Music series (2001). *Music: The Accordions of Puhoi* (1996), transcribed by Roger Buckton. For further discussion see Buckton, *Bohemian Journey* (2013), pp. 18, 19. See also p. 148.

D'Wawa sitzt in da Hennastoll aaf de Stånga
u da Herri kua(n)'s niat dalånga.

Granny sits in the hen house on the perch
and Grandfather can't reach her.

Tony Bayer

Wenn me Voda wart a Stullitz g'west
und ma Mutta a Zeiseri,
döi löiwa Wirtschoft höit i gern g'sea,
in Vuogerlhaisl.

If my father would have been a goldfinch
and my mother a siskin,
I would have liked to see this business,
in the bird cage.

Tony Bayer

Opposite: Chotěšov was the home town of the Bayer family. Known as Chotieschau in 1863, when the official language was German, it is dominated by this abbey, formerly a nunnery founded in 1202. *Michael Cwach*

Above: Anton (Tony) Bayer (left) with Egerlander Matthias Baumann and dudelsack in 1984. *PHS 0411*

5.
Songs about feelings and relationships

Bist denn du bäis?

Are you angry?

Literal translations from Deitsch

English

Are you angry or don't you hear, don't you hear?
Are you angry or don't you hear?

I am not angry and I hear you yet, hear you yet
I am not angry and I hear you yet.

High German

Bist denn du böse oder hörst du nicht, hörst du nicht?
Bist denn du böse oder hörst du nicht?

Ich bin nicht böse und ich höre dich schon, höre dich schon,
Ich bin nicht böse und ich höre dich schon.

Notes

Bist denn du bäis? was recorded by Werner Droescher during the centennial celebrations at Pūhoi in 1963. After an accordion introduction, both verses were sung clearly by an unidentified male singer. Published versions of this song include extra verses. Bergmann (1952) and Sykora (1976) provide the context and story behind the song, see p. 148.

SOURCES *Text and music:* From a recording by Werner Droescher (1963), transcribed by Ralf Heimrath and Roger Buckton. See also p. 148.

| The musicians on stage at the centennial celebrations in 1963. *PHS 1329*

Za di bin i gånga

To you did I venture

Literal translations from Deitsch

English

I went to you and I was pleased to be with you,

I'll never more go to you, the way is too far for me.

The mountain is too high for me and the people are too snobbish.

I will not go to you anymore, the way is too far for me.

High German

Zu dir bin ich gegangen und zu dir hat (es) mich gefreut,

Zu dir gehe ich nicht mehr, der Weg ist mir zu weit.

Der Berg ist mir zu hoch und die Leute sind mir zu geschwollen.

Zu dir komme ich nicht mehr, der Weg ist mir zu weit.

Notes

Za di bin i gånga was a well-known song and the community sang it heartily in the Pūhoi hall at the 1963 celebrations. Fred Rauner remembered most of it in his interview with Judith Williams in 2017 and Werner Droescher's informants pieced the text together but without remembering the tune. Versions of the song are known in Egerland, Böhmerwald, Austria and Bavaria. Some of these versions show the song as a gentle lullaby, three beats to the bar and a yodelling-type chorus; for example, *Singendes Egerland* (1976). However, the recorded versions of the community singing at Pūhoi in 1963 and Fred Rauner in 2017 clearly demonstrate that it is a rather jaunty song in 4/4 time (as in the music opposite), and this is further confirmed by Droescher who noted it as a polka.

SOURCES *Text and music:* recordings of community singing (Droescher, 1963) and Fred Rauner (Buckton, 2017), transcribed by Ralf Heimrath and Roger Buckton; Brosch (1997), *Singendes Egerland* (1976). *Informants:* Don and Anton Bayer, Judith Williams collection. See also p. 149, 150.

The watercolour 'Sunset on the Puhoi River' (also known as 'Wenderholm') was painted in 1880 by Alfred Sharpe. It depicts the coastal landscape around the time the early Bohemian settlers arrived. *The Fletcher Trust Collection*

Duarl haot g'sågt

Dora has said

Ben Straka's version (1984)

Literal translations from Deitsch

English

Dora has said, Dora has said,
the plums are good,
let's pick them up,
let's pick them up,
let's put them into the hat.

Dora has said, Dora has said,
today we have winter,
I am too old, I am too old,
I can bear no children.

High German

Dora hat gesagt, Dora hat gesagt,
die Zwetschgen sind gut,
klauben wir sie zusammen,
klauben wir sie zusammen,
tun wir sie in den Hut.

Dora hat gesagt, Dora hat gesagt,
heute haben wir Winter,
ich bin schon zu alt, ich bin schon zu alt,
bekomme keine Kinder.

Ben Straka (left) farewelling Erich Baumann at the end of the Egerlanders' visit to Pūhoi in 1984. In front of them is May Wenzlick. *PHS 0579*

Duarl haot g’sågt

Dora has said

Fred Rauner’s version (2017)

Literal translations from Deitsch

English	*High German*
Dora has said, Dora has said,	Dora hat gesagt, Dora hat gesagt,
the pine cones are good,	die kleinen Pinienzapfen sind gut,
let’s pick them up,	klauben wir sie zusammen,
let’s pick them up,	klauben wir sie zusammen,
let’s put them into the hat.	tun wir sie in den Hut.

Notes

During the Egerlanders’ visit to Pūhoi in 1984,[8] Erich Baumann recorded Ben Straka singing this song and published it in a collection entitled *Egerländer Volkslieder* (Egerland Folksongs) in 1990. This same song was also collected and recorded from Fred Rauner by Judith Williams and Roger Buckton in 2017. This text was subsequently transcribed by Ralf Heimrath.

Although there are two verses in the Straka version, it is evident that Fred Rauner had not learned or remembered a second verse. When Ralf Heimrath was in New Zealand in 2018, he met Fred and they had a conversation in the dialect for about an hour. (Later, each praised the other on his command of the language!)

The melody and texts of these two versions are slightly different and demonstrate how a folksong can change over a relatively brief period (there are 33 years between the Straka and Rauner versions) and be sung in different ways from person to person. The change in the melody is typical of these Bohemian tunes being 'anglicised', with the smoothing over of the melodic line and giving it a lilt by 'dotting' the faster notes.

Ben Straka's version innocently commends plums in verse one but incorporates issues of fertility in the second verse (see p. 151 for more details). Fred Rauner, on the other hand, sings of the goodness of *Boutzala* (pine cones).

Imagine the prevalence of conifers and pine cones in central Europe in the 19th century. Children gathered the cones in their thousands and families used them for fires and stoves, especially in the cold winter months. The hearty crackle of the burning cones would have been an evocative sound and their shape and form meant they were perfect on the Christmas tree with apples and candles. The cones could be painted and decorated, and used as toys — so *Boutzala san gout*!

At Pūhoi, then surrounded by the New Zealand bush, there were no pine cones (except arguably the cones of the kauri, and the less common kaikawaka and kawaka, the only native conifers to produce woody cones that split open when mature). It would have taken a few decades for their familiar European conifers to be established so there were no *Boutzala*, yet the song continued to be sung as a memory of the old country.

SOURCES *Text and music:* Interview with Ben Straka in 1984 by Erich Baumann (1990, p. 35); recording from an interview with Fred Rauner by Judith Williams and Roger Buckton (2017), transcribed by Ralf Heimrath and Roger Buckton; recording Werner Droescher (1963). *Informants:* Joe Tolhopf, Steve Straka, Tony Bayer, Judith Williams collection. See also p. 151.

Porcelain Christmas mugs featuring the traditional pine cone motif are still popular in Bohemia. These were fired by Czech company Bohemia Porcelain in 2024.

Der wos döi bayrisch Duadl will hom

Who wants Bavarian Dora must have

Literal translations from Deitsch

English

Who wants to have Dora from Bavaria,
he must wear a little velvet cap.
A little velvet cap and silver shoe buckles,
that will well please Dora from Bavaria.

High German

Wer die bayrische Duarl haben will,
der muss ein samtenes Mützchen aufhaben.
Ein samtenes Mützchen und silberne Schuhschnallen,
das wird der bayrischen Duarl schon gefallen.

Notes

Der wos döi bayrisch Duadl was sung to Judith Williams by Joseph Tolhopf. She notated the text but not the music, but this same text with a melody was found in the Gubernial Collection by Thomas Kunz.[9] Dated 1825 — just 38 years before the Bohemian settlers first went to Pūhoi — it can perhaps be fairly assumed that the melody above is an accurate realisation from the 19th century (though of course it may have changed since arriving in New Zealand).

The rhythm is an example of mixed metre, changing from duple time (two beats to the bar) to triple time (three beats to the bar) every two bars. There is a charm about these Bohemian mixed-metre songs and dances, but they did not suit the English colonial dances and so were among the first to be forgotten. Compare this song with *Gickerl, wennst du niat krahst,* p. 36.

This is a song of social class: Dora will not marry a peasant, but is looking for someone who wears a velvet cap and silver-buckled shoes!

SOURCES *Text:* Informant Joe Tolhopf, Judith Williams collection. *Music:* Kunz (1825), p. 40. See also p. 151.

Ben Straka sporting his velvet cap (c. 1980s), but perhaps not seeking Bavarian Dora! *PHS 4787*

Dra Åckarla Kraat

Three cabbage fields

Literal translations from Deitsch

English	*High German*
Three small fields with cabbage,	Drei Äckerlein Kraut,
three fields with turnips,	drei Äckerlein Rüben,
the prettier the girls,	je schöner die Mädchen,
the more liked by the boys.	desto lieber haben sie Buben.
Three small fields with cabbage,	Drei Äckerlein Kraut,
three fields with turnips,	drei Äckerlein Rüben,
who wants to have my girl,	wer mein schönes Mädchen haben will,
needs to sweet-talk.	muss schmeicheln können.

Erich Baumann playing the violin with Laurie Rauner on accordion in 1984, while Anton (Tony) Bayer looks on. *PHS 0366*

Notes

In 1984 there was a most successful cultural exchange between a party of Bohemians from Pūhoi and an Egerland group from Bavaria, Germany. One of the leaders of the Egerland group was the well-known and highly respected musician Erich Baumann. He collected this Pūhoi song from Laurie Rauner, the leader of the Puhoi Bohemian Band, and published it in a collection entitled *Egerländer Volkslieder* (1990). Three fields of cabbages and three fields of turnips are the dowry for the farmer's pretty daughter. Cabbage (Kraut) and turnips are common in the Egerland and Bavaria.

SOURCES *Text and music:* interview with Laurie Rauner in 1984 by Erich Baumann (1985), pp. 34, 35. See also p. 151.

Meck, meck, d'Zeng is gfreckt

Meh, meh, the goat is dead

Medley: Däi Schul håst du ålla aaf dia

The blame is all on you

Literal translations from Deitsch

English	*High German*
Meh, meh, the goat is dead,	Meck, meck, die Ziege ist tot,
and the goat buck lies there as well.	Und der Geißbock liegt halt auch dort.
Now I don't know,	Jetzt weiß ich nicht,
Whether to hang him or drown him.	erhänge ich ihn nur oder ertränke ich ihn nur.
The blame is all on you, you,	Die Schuld hast du alle auf dir, dir,
Because you are being so false to me.	Weil du so falsch mit mir umgehst.

Notes

This song is one of the most interesting in the collection as an example of how many of these songs were collected and restored. The first two lines were included in Judith Williams's collection, as sung by Rosie Schischka, but they were the only words remembered. Later, in an interview in 2017, Fred Rauner plucked out of memory the version shown here. He sang clearly but what he sang seemed to lack musical coherence. He was asked if he played it on the accordion, but he didn't think so.

Then, in 2023, Ralf Heimrath made the connection with the piece *Däi Schul håst du ålla aaf dia* (*The blame is all on you*) as recorded on *Die Booei Musikgruppe* (Band 3), with *Ha(n)sl Bou* (p. 56) following. In the second half of Fred Rauner's song he is singing an almost identical melody to the accordion tune on the CD and his text at that point is exactly the same as the name of the piece *Däi Schul håst du ålla aaf dia*. Fred said he used to sing it with Kenny Wech. It was well known that the Wechs kept goats, and the text about the state of the goats could be a metaphor for a human relationship (and the second half of the song clearly states where the blame lies!). This may, in fact, be two songs and Fred Rauner, or his source, linked them deliberately or subconsciously.

Meck, meck, d'Zeng is gfreckt as Rauner sang it concludes at bar 14, overlapping the Puhoi Band version which starts at bar 8. Perhaps there was text from bar 15 onwards. Musicians may note that the phrases from bar 15 to the end do not follow the usual 8-bar phrase length, but that is how it was recorded and played three times on the CD.

The melody of *Däi Schul håst du ålla aaf dia* is also in the Charles Becher manuscript book but it is unnamed there. It appears in the middle of a waltz melody, *Wooden shoe waltz*. Unlike the Puhoi Band recording, the following song, *Ha(n)sl Bou*, is not another tune in medley as it appears in the Becher book, and this perhaps supports the view that the old dialect songs were put together for dance medleys by various Pūhoi musicians according to their taste at the time. Neither of these songs/pieces have been discovered in European sources. Perhaps they were lost to European folk music, but it is also possible that they were composed in New Zealand and in the dialect.

SOURCES *Text and music:* Recordings of the Puhoi Band (1993) and from an interview with Fred Rauner by Judith Williams and Roger Buckton (2017), transcribed by Ralf Heimrath and Roger Buckton. *Music manuscript:* Charles Becher manuscript book. *Informant:* Judith Williams collection. See also p. 152.

Du bist a schäi(n)s Moidl,
Du bist a gouts Moidl,
Sa mei Moidl bist du niat.

You are a pretty girl,
You are a good girl,
but you are not my girl.

A rhyme from Jimmy Bayer

Werner Droescher milking a goat, c. 1962. The name of the person behind him is not known. *Werner Otto Droescher papers. 1962–1978. MSS & Archives. Special Collections, University of Auckland Libraries and Learning Services.*

Ha(n)sl Bou

Johnny boy

Joseph Russek waltz

Literal translations from Deitsch

English	*High German*
Johnny boy, Johnny boy,	Hanslbub, Hanslbub,
take the pretty Eva.	nimm die schöne Eva.
She has nice high-heeled shoes	Hat sie schöne Stöckelschuhe
and beautiful roses.	und schöne Röslein.
Johnny boy, Johnny boy,	Hanslbub, Hanslbub,
take the pretty Eva.	nimm die schöne Eva.
She has nice pinafores	Hat sie schöne Kittelchen
and pretty aprons.	und schöne Schürzen.

Notes

The text offers advice to the young Hansl (Johnny) that he should marry Eva because she has high-heeled shoes, roses, nice gowns and beautiful pinafores. In other words, this is an opportunity for social betterment!

Ha(n)sl Bou is another song collected by Erich Baumann during the visit of the Egerlanders in 1984 and later published in *Egerländer Volkslieder* (1990), where he notes the sources as 19th century, from Pūhoi and Tachau (Czech Republic). It is also in the Gubernial Collection.[10] The song informant was Tony Bayer and it appears that Bayer may have provided the second verse.

Following the song is an instrumental section. In the colonial setting in Pūhoi, this medley was used for dancing a waltz played by instruments — most likely violin and accordion. It was named the *Joseph Russek waltz* after one of the early settlers at Pūhoi, perhaps Joseph Russek, son of 1863 pioneers Anton and Margarethe Russek, but because of the timing it is more likely that it was Joseph's and his wife Catherine's (Plescher) son Joseph Vincent Russek (1895–1983). It is this version that is in the Becher manuscript book and played by the Puhoi Band (1993).

In *Egerländer Volkslieder* Baumann shows bars 17–32 as a 'Zwischenspiel' (an interlude), but perhaps it was a known song in the 19th century. Bars 33–42 are an obvious repetition of the *Ha(n)sl Bou* melody and, as noted by Baumann, bars 42–61 are a variant of *Dra Åckarla Kraat* (p. 50).

SOURCES *Text:* From the recording by Werner Droescher (1963), transcribed by Ralf Heimrath. *Music:* From an interview with Anton Bayer in 1984, transcribed by Erich Baumann (1990), pp. 34, 35; Charles Becher manuscript book; Puhoi Band CD (1993), transcribed by Roger Buckton. *Informants:* Christina Wech, Annie Rauner, Alice and Anton Bayer, Judith Williams collection. See p. 152.

Joseph Russek (1852–1917) and Catherine Russek (née Plescher, 1866–1943) c. 1900.
PHS 5671a

View of the Pūhoi School (centre) and village with the steamship *Kotiti* on the river (c. 1900). *Alexander Turnbull Library 1/2-000153-G William Archer Price*

Education and schools

The early settlers had experienced schooling in village schools in Bohemia, which were well-established and ahead of what was being provided in England. Children learned both Czech and German at school and teachers in Bohemia were appointed on the basis of their music qualifications.[11] Many served as both school teacher and musician for the village or town.

On the arrival of the first small group of Bohemians at Pūhoi in 1863, classes for the children were almost immediately set up in one of the whare provided by the government for the new settlers to use as shelter. The children were taught by Mrs Emily Krippner, an Englishwoman married to the man who encouraged his Bohemian compatriots to settle at Pūhoi, Martin Krippner.

By 1872, local men John Schollum and John Wenzlick petitioned the government to erect a school in Pūhoi. The Board of Education agreed to advance £80 provided the settlers would subscribe another £80. John Schollum had made a tour of the district and found that five families could donate £1 each, while others

Above: Josef Navrátil (1798–1865) painted this scene in 1857, six years before the settlers left for Pūhoi. From Bohemia, it illustrates the importance attached to music in the village schools at the time. Could this account for the musical skills of the musicians from Pūhoi and Ōhaupō?

Left above: The new Pūhoi convent school, opened in 1923. *PHS 0297*

Left below: The convent school closed in the 1960s due to falling rolls. Today it is home to the Puhoi Heritage Museum and the Puhoi Playgroup. *Roger Buckton*

contributed shillings. Despite this effort, only £65 was raised. Schollum then wrote to his father in Bohemia, who sent the £15 shortfall along with his other two sons, who came with the next batch of emigrants to arrive in 1872. The school was then built.

Successive bishops and priests of the Pūhoi parish had also attempted to establish a convent school. They had initially met with resistance, possibly because for centuries there had been little choice but to work for the Chotieschau convent (see p. 38) and support the nuns there. The chance to own their own land and make their own choices was the main incentive for many of the Bohemians to immigrate to New Zealand.

At a meeting of parishioners in August 1922, Father Silk challenged them to build a convent school as a perpetual monument to their faith, and by the end of the meeting all the parishioners were in favour. Charlie Becher was engaged as the builder.

At the beginning of the 1923 school year, the convent school was ready to receive 73 pupils. The motto 'Gratia et Veritas' — grace and truth — was added to the white-painted exterior and Sisters of the Order of St Joseph, Cletus and Pelagi were engaged as teachers, including a music teacher and junior mistress. A large villa was soon built for their home.

A high standard of education was provided at the school and regular concerts were presented in the village hall and sports visits arranged with other schools. However, by 1964 the numbers of children attending had fallen and the decision was made to close the convent school. The school building continues to serve the community, being the home of the Puhoi Playgroup and the Puhoi Heritage Museum.

Jenny Schollum

6. Singing with their children

Wiewadl, wawadl, was is das?

Weiwadl, wawadl, what is that?

Literal translations from Deitsch

English

Weiwadl, wawadl, what is that?
Behind the manger something is crawling.
It's not a hare and not a fox.
Weiwadl, wawadl, what is that?

Weiwadl, wawadl, what is that?
Behind the forest something is crawling.
It's not a dog and it's not a sow.
Weiwadl, wawadl, what is that?

High German

Wiewadl, wawadl, was ist das?
Hinter dem Stall da krabbelt was.
Es ist kein Hase und ist kein Fuchs.
Wiewadl, wawadl, was ist das?

Wiewadl, wawadl, was ist das?
Hinter dem Forst drüben krabbelt was.
Es ist kein Hund und ist keine Sau.
Wiewadl, wawadl, was ist das?

Notes

Wiewadl, wawadl is also known in Pūhoi as 'Wee little Granny'. A fun action song for young children, it is a good tune on button accordion. Two text variations were collected from Werner Droescher and Fred Rauner and each has been used for verses 1 and 2. There are other text variations from north and south Egerland. These show an awareness of the rhyme: for example, lines 1 (*das*) and 3 (*Hase*) could have been achieved in verse 1 by swapping *Hase* (bunny) and *Fuchs* (fox). It seems that this may not have been a priority with the mothers of Pūhoi, or perhaps our singer's memory was at fault.

SOURCES *Text:* Recording of verse 1 (Droescher, 1963), verse 2 Fred Rauner (Buckton, 2017), transcribed by Ralf Heimrath. *Music recording:* Fred Rauner (2017) and Pūhoi Band (1993), recorded by Roger Buckton. *Informant:* From Werner Droescher (1963), Judith Williams collection. See also p. 152.

Unna Vetta Veitl

Little Cousin Veitl

Literal translations from Deitsch

English

Our cousin Veitl
wants to become a cavalryman.
He doesn't have a shako yet,
so he can't become one.
His mother takes a dumpling pot,
puts it on Veitl's head.
Ride Veitl, ride!
Ride Veitl, ride!

High German

Unser Vetter Veitl
will ein Reiter werden.
Hat er noch keinen Tschako,
kann er keiner werden.
Nimmt seine Mutter einen Knödeltopf,
setzt ihn dem Veitl auf den Kopf.
Reite Veitl, reite!
Reite Veitl, reite!

Notes

Unna Vetta Veitl is a song for young children that was collected by Judith Williams from Don and Anton Bayer. The melody, with similar words, was located in the published collection by Albert Brosch (1986). Different versions invent other apparel that Veitl is missing; for example, boots (see Song origins, p. 152). 'Vetta' means kinsman, a relative, and in Egerland it can also mean any member of the adult male community, similar to when a speaker addresses an English speaker as 'Brother'.

SOURCES *Text:* Informants Don and Anton Bayer, Judith Williams collection. *Music:* Albert Brosch (1986). See also p. 152.

Albert Brosch

Albert Brosch (1886–1970) was a German master watchmaker, but it is as a folk-song collector that he is now remembered. During his working life, he collected over 2300 songs, children's dances, rhymes, ditties and games and these were published posthumously in four volumes, *Der Liederschatz des Egerlandes* (1986). Four of the songs in this collection (pp. 42, 46, 64, 83) were collected by Brosch in the late 1930s from the region of the Egerland homelands of the Pūhoi settlers. That over 2000 songs were collected points to the enthusiasm of the Egerlanders for singing and their culture. Brosch wrote that these Egerlanders are the truest adherents to the old customs, dialects and folksongs and that it would hurt an Egerlander in his soul if one of 'his' songs were sung in High German.

Albert Brosch, c. 1950s, was a German watchmaker and folksong collector. From *Eger und das Egerland*

Children's rhymes

A-B-C, d'Katz laaft übern Schnee

A-B-C,
d'Katz laaft übern Schnee,
hot sie schäina weißa Schäichala ua,
Laaft sie bis aaf Rückazua(n)

A-B-C,
the cat is running over the snow,
she has pretty little white shoes on,
she runs until she comes to Rokycan.

Annie Schischka

Daamanickl, Breialekl

Daamanickl,
Breialekl,
Longa Hons,
Fingaringerl,
Christkindl.

Little thumb,
Mash licker,
Long John,
Little ring finger,
Christ Child.

Laurie and Ben Straka

Left to right: Annie Schischka with her mother, Theresia Straka, and sister, Rosie Gobbie, c. 1960s. *PHS 5338*

Schousta, Schousta flick

(This is a rhyme for when a child rides on someone's knee)

Schousta, Schousta, flick,
d'Noudl is zu dick,
d'Noudl is zu g'krummp,
da Schousta is a retta Lump.

Shoemaker, shoemaker, sew,
the needle is too thick,
the needle is too crooked,
the shoemaker is a proper rogue.

Annie Schischka

Customs and festive days

The rhythm of the year for the Bohemians was dictated by the weather and the church. Of course, New Zealand was the reverse of Europe as far as seasonal festivals were concerned, but the Catholic calendar provided a familiar framework of feast and saint days.

Just before Easter (spring in northern Europe), there was a custom in Egerland in which a group of young girls would go around the village holding a little green tree (known as 'Maia') from which a pillow holding a puppet (symbolising a baby) hung. The standing girl says or sings that the baby breathes like a dudelsack.

The Maia folk tradition is represented on a tile from a decorative porcelain stove by Willy Russ (1888–1974) now housed in the Muzeum Cheb, Czech Republic. The stove was made between 1938 and 1943 and depicts scenes of Egerland customs and folklore from an earlier era. *Muzeum Cheb*

Haio bobaio

(similar to hush-a-bye baby)
Haio bobaio,
samma gelta Maia,
wenn döi Lait herumgeah,
mou ii bai da Wicka steah,
niich — nooch, niich — nooch,
dea schlaft, man(n) kloina dicka Dudlsooch.

Haio bobaio,
we are 'Maia', aren't we? [Maia girls]
when these people are going around,
I have to stand with the doll [in a pillow]
nich — noch, nich — noch,
[sound of a loudly breathing child]
he's sleeping, my little fat dudelsack.

Alma Schischka and Gretchen Elizabeth
'Bibby' Cotter née Williams

7.
Fun and satire

In d'Stod eifoahrn

To town, let's start

Literal translations from Deitsch

English

To go to town, to go to town,
in our old tumbrel cart.

The innkeeper from Luhe sold his house
and bought his wife a little hat,
a little hat, with a posie on it,
she wears it every Sunday.

High German

In die Stadt hineinfahren, in die Stadt
hineinfahren,
mit unserem alten Schinderkarren.

Der Wirt von Luhe hat das Haus verkauft
und seiner Alten ein Hütchen gekauft,
ein Hütchen gekauft, ein Sträußchen drauf,
das setzt sie alle Sonntage auf.

Notes

How many of us remember a tune but have forgotten the words? This tune is in the waltz medley *Summer Air in May* (p. 28). The words are known in the Upper Palatine (an administrative district in east Bavaria) and have provided the text for our song.

SOURCES *Text:* Published in Eichenseer/Karrer (1999), p. 69. *Music:* Charles Becher manuscript book and Puhoi Band (1993), transcribed by Roger Buckton. See also p. 153.

Schwaza Pfaala raid i ge(r)an

Riding small black mares I like

Pohuehue Polka

Literal translations from Deitsch

English

I like to ride black (little) horses
and much more brown (little) horses.
I like my mother-in-law
and the daughter much more.

My girl has a white belly
with a black fleck.
I've brushed it the whole night
and could not remove the fleck.

But my girl told me,
laughingly that,
a hundred others
could not remove it as well!

High German

Schwarze Pferdchen reite ich gern
und Füchslein noch viel lieber.
Meine Schwiegermutter habe ich gern
und die Tochter noch viel lieber.

Mein Mädchen hat'n weißen Bauch
und drauf ein' schwarzen Fleck.
Ich hab' die ganze Nacht geputzt
und bring den Fleck nicht weg.

Mein Mädchen aber sagte mir,
und hat dabei gelacht,
es hätten hundert andere
den Fleck nicht weggebracht!

Notes

All of Werner Droescher's informants seemed to know most of the first verse of this song but perhaps as a rhyme. However, the tune of *Pohuehue polka* could be vaguely discerned and these verses exactly matched *Pohuehue polka* as notated in Charles Becher's manuscript book (spelled Pohuihui).

Verses 2 and 3 have been taken from a version of the same song from Saxony and transcribed into the Egerland dialect by Ralf Heimrath. Of course, it is not known whether these verses were sung in Pūhoi, but they have been included because they enhance the character and provide a more substantial song for performance purposes. Its erotic nature requires a twinkle in the eye and a lightness of touch!

The *Pohuehue polka* was named after a rugged area just out of Pūhoi, home of the Wech family. It is now a scenic reserve, with bush walks and waterfalls. Pohuehue is the Māori name for the native shrub *Muehlenbeckia complexa*.

SOURCES *Text and music:* Verse 1, recording by Werner Droescher (1963), transcribed by Ralf Heimrath and Roger Buckton. *Music:* Charles Becher manuscript book. Verses 2 and 3, author unknown, from Saxony in the north of Egerland. See also p. 153.

O du löiwa Augustin

O my dear friend Augustin

Literal translations from Deitsch

English	*High German*
O my dear friend Augustin, Augustin, Augustin,	O du lieber Augustin, Augustin, Augustin,
o my dear friend Augustin, all has gone.	o du lieber Augustin, alles ist hin.
Money gone, honey gone.	Geld ist weg, Mäd'l ist weg.
All has gone, all has gone.	Alles weg, alles weg.
O my dear friend Augustin, all has gone.	O du lieber Augustin, alles ist hin.
O my dear friend Augustin, Augustin, Augustin,	O du lieber Augustin, Augustin, Augustin,
o my dear friend Augustin, all has gone.	o du lieber Augustin, alles ist hin.
Coat has gone, cane has gone,	Rock ist weg, Stock ist weg,
Augustin lies in mud.	Augustin liegt im Dreck.
O my dear friend Augustin, all has gone.	O du lieber Augustin, alles ist hin.

Notes

Annie Rauner sang this song on a cassette recording for her niece Dorothy Berger, who gave it to Roger Buckton in 1993. As memory of the text in the dialect began to fade, she reverted to the English text of the young children's song with the same tune, 'The more we are together, the happier we will be'. This is quite different in spirit to the Augustin text, which refers to a poor dudelsack player in 17th-century Vienna falling drunk into the gutter and then being thrown into a plague pit. The story continues with Augustin playing his dudelsack in the pit and startling a passer-by, who presumably rescued him. It was also recorded by the Puhoi Band in 1993 and entitled *Liebe Augustine*.

SOURCES *Text and music recording:* Annie Rauner collected by Dorothy Berger; text transcribed and completed from a publication from Vienna (c. 1800) by Ralf Heimrath; music recording Puhoi Band (1993), transcribed by Roger Buckton. See also p. 152.

Wenn häit ma(n) Mutta ma(n) Huasn niat g'flickt

So if my mother hadn't sewn my pants

Literal translations from Deitsch

English

If my mother hadn't sewn my
trousers,
I would have gone in only my shirt, etc.
If my mother hadn't sewn my
trousers,
I would have gone in only my shirt, etc.

High German

Wenn meine Mutter meine Hose nicht
geflickt hätte,
dann wäre ich im Hemd gegangen, etc.
Wenn meine Mutter meine Hose nicht
geflickt hätte,
dann wäre ich im Hemd gegangen, etc.

Notes

When *Wenn häit ma(n) Mutta* was sung at the centennial celebrations in 1963, the whole hall sang it heartily. It is in the *Schedewy polka* (p. 30) and the Puhoi Band recorded it in 1993 using the full name of the song and adding a short instrumental coda (bars 17–24). This coda rounds off the total number of bars to 24 — more suitable for dancing the polka.

The tune can be found in Egerland sources, but there is not the repetition of the text stanzas, suggesting that, over the years, some of the original text has been forgotten by the Pūhoi singers. This same tune in Czech is used for the song *Proč se ty hájové zelenají* (Why are the groves turning green?). Various versions can be found online.

SOURCES *Text and music:* From the recording by Werner Droescher (1963), transcribed by Ralf Heimrath and Roger Buckton. *Music recording:* Puhoi Band (1993), recorded by Roger Buckton. *Music manuscript:* Charles Becher manuscript book. See also p. 153, 154.

8.
Drinking songs

Gsundhait mainer und Gsundhait dainer

My good health and your good health

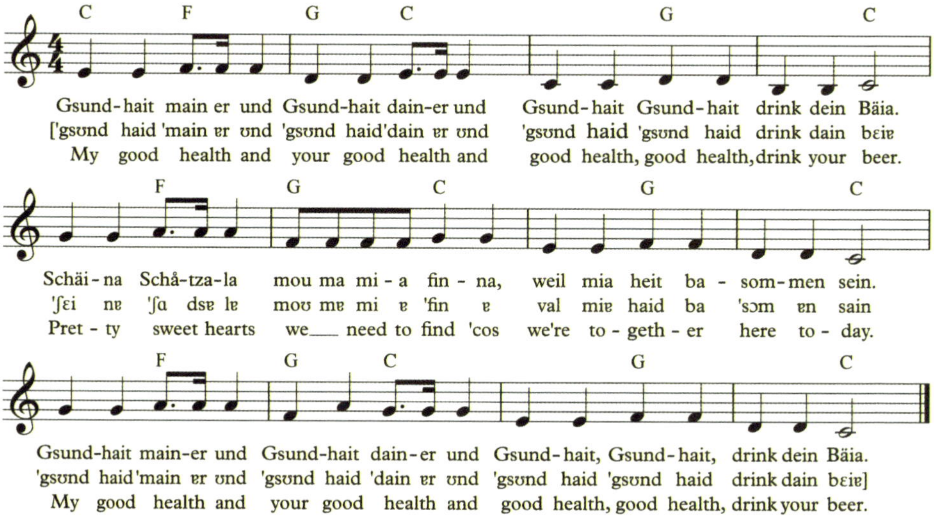

Literal translations from Deitsch

English

Good health to me, good health to you,
good health, good health, drink your beer.
We need to find pretty sweethearts,
because we are together today.
Good health to me, good health to you,
good health, good health, drink your beer.

High German

Gesundheit mir und Gesundheit dir,
Gesundheit, Gesundheit, trink dein Bier.
Schöne Schätzchen müssen wir finden,
weil wir heute beisammen sind.
Gesundheit mir und Gesundheit dir,
Gesundheit, Gesundheit, trink dein Bier.

Notes

Bohemians are famous for their beer, particularly the Pilsen style. Chotieschau (now Chotěšov in the Czech Republic) and neighbouring villages (p. 100), where many of the Pūhoi settlers originated, are all in the wider district of Pilsen. The Puhoi Hotel was one of the first and most important buildings in Pūhoi and, together with the church and local hall, remains that way today.

The *Spectrum* podcast from RNZ (*Spectrum* was a documentary series which ran from 1972 to 2016) features a recording made in the Puhoi Hotel in 1976, and this was used to provide the text and music reproduced here. This drinking song is a classic and is still sung throughout most of German-speaking Europe. The music is also used for a Pūhoi dance, the *Prince of Wales Schottischer* (see also p. 90).

The text is very old: the grammatical form *Gesundheit mainer und Gesundheit dainer* is not used today. Legend has it that when the Bohemian settlers were on their way across Europe by train, they stayed overnight at the port of Altona, Hamburg (where Werner Droescher was a student at a teachers' college 67 years later) before catching the ship to London and then on to New Zealand. It was the Prince of Wales's birthday at that time (the Prince of Wales being Prince Albert Edward, eldest son of Queen Victoria and Prince Albert of Saxe-Coburg and Gotha) and it was in Hamburg that they learned the *Prince of Wales Schottischer*.

SOURCES *Text and music:* From the *Spectrum* documentary broadcast (later made into a podcast) by RNZ (1976); Ben Straka recorded by his son, Gerard Straka; interview with Fred Rauner by Judith Williams and Roger Buckton (2017), text transcribed by Ralf Heimrath and music by Roger Buckton. *Informants:* Laurie Rauner, Steve Straka, Adam Rauner and Anton Bayer, Judith Williams collection.

The Pūhoi pub: good health and drink your beer

The four drinking songs in this collection attest to a strong relationship between alcohol and the vocal cords! These dialect songs were sung in the taverns of the Egerland region and then shipped to Pūhoi by means of the minds and memory of the men who sang them. How long these songs lasted in the community is not known, but it is significant that Jack Perkins's RNZ *Spectrum* documentary on Pūhoi, broadcast in 1976, opened with the song *Gsundhait mainer*, recorded in the Pūhoi pub.

The home town of many of the settlers, Chotieschau, is in the administrative district of Pilsen. The famous Pilsener lager was developed here in 1842. It is doubtful that any of the settlers brought a Pilsener with them in 1863 but we can be sure that many have been drunk at the Pūhoi pub since that time.

The iconic image of the pub, especially on a Sunday afternoon, is well known but it was the characterful inner rooms which provided the atmosphere for music-making.

Opposite above: A group of men outside the first Pūhoi pub, c. late 1870s, possibly after a wedding. The only woman, Elizabeth Schollum, is in the doorway. *PHS 1150a*

Opposite below: The hotel at Pūhoi in 1963 during the centennial celebrations, a time when many of the songs featured in this book were recorded. *PHS 0225*

BAR

PUHOI HOTEL

I u ma(n ålts Wei

Me and my old wife

Literal translations from Deitsch

English

Me and my old wife can dance well.
She with the beggar's bag, I with the knapsack.
Diddle, doodle, daddle, schrum, schrum, schrum, here comes the polka again.
Me and my old wife, we can dance well.

She goes every day to town and she has to walk.
What she has begged, I waste it on drink.
When she comes here with her begging-bag,
I take all that she has begged.
Hooray, that's what I take into the pub.

High German

Ich und mein altes Weib können schön tanzen.
Sie mit dem Bettelsack, ich mit dem Ranzen.
Didl, dudl, dadl, schrum, schrum, schrum, geht schon der Hopser 'rum.
Ich und mein altes Weib tanzen schön zu.

Sie geht jeden Tag in die Stadt, da muss sie laufen.
Was sie erbettelt hat, tu ich versaufen.
Wenn sie kommt mit ihrem Bettelsack,
nehm' ich, was sie erbettelt hat.
Heißa, das trag' ich gleich ins Wirtshaus rein.

Notes

This delightful song has been reconstructed from scanty beginnings. Werner Droescher collected just the text of the first verse in 1963. However, this text is quite well known in Egerland, and both the text and music can be found in key collections such as Brosch (1997) and Baumann (1990). Baumann references the song as being collected in 1913 in Tachau (Czech Republic).

Perhaps the first verse is all the Pūhoi people sang. If this is so, it is a rather repetitive and short song — just one phrase of four bars repeated. After consideration, our attention turned to another German folksong, *Heißa Kathreinerle*. This song has the same melody but it also has two more phrases of music and text for each verse (line 3) and the addition of these makes sense in terms of completing the song texturally and musically. However, since *Heißa Kathreinerle* dates from 1928, it should be omitted from authentic Pūhoi music performances.

SOURCES *Text:* From recording by Werner Droescher (1963), transcribed by Ralf Heimrath. *Text and music:* From Brosch (1986), collected Eger in 1937; Baumann (1990), collected Tachau in 1913. *Informants:* From Droescher (1963), Judith Williams collection. See also p. 154.

Hans gaih huom

Hans go home

Literal translations from Deitsch

English

John go home,
you don't know what the weather will be.
It could be raining or snowing,
tomorrow morning you will rue it.
John go home, John stay here.

High German

Hans, geh heim,
du weißt ja nicht wie das Wetter wird.
Es könnte regnen, könnte auch schneien,
morgen früh wird es dich reuen.
Hans geh heim, Hans bleib da.

Notes

When Werner Droescher recorded community singing at Pūhoi in 1963, everyone knew these words. Still popular in southern Germany as a pub song, Hans (or John) wants to go home to his wife but his friends remonstrate that it is better to stay at the pub and that he is a hen-pecked husband. Only one verse was recorded in Pūhoi, but other verses sung in Europe make this meaning clear. The tune is used in the instrumental medley *Schedewy Polka* (p. 30).

SOURCES *Text and music:* From the recordings by Werner Droescher and Puhoi Hall community singing (1963), Fred Rauner (2017), Puhoi Band (1993), transcribed by Judith Williams and Roger Buckton. *Music:* Charles Becher manuscript book. *Informant:* Alice Bayer, Judith Williams collection. See also p. 156, 158.

Four dudelsacks at the Pūhoi hall on 26 June 1999. Back row (dudelsacks): David Krippner, Ian Whyman, Dianne Barnes and Roger Buckton. Front row: Dot Berger (accordion), Linda Hill (violin), Fred Rauner (accordion) and Laurie Rauner (accordion). *Christine Krippner*

A Räuscherl im Kopf

I'm merry and tipsy

Literal translations from Deitsch

English

A bit tipsy in the head and my honey with me,
my honey with me, my honey with me,
are we dancing and turning around in a swarm,
around in a swarm, in a swarm.

High German

Beschwipst im Kopf und mein Mädchen am Arm,
mein Mädchen am Arm, mein Mädchen am Arm,
gehn wir tanzen und dreh'n uns herum in dem Schwarm,
herum in dem Schwarm, in dem Schwarm.

Notes

This is the final tune in the *Summer Air in May waltz* medley (p. 28) as transcribed in the Charles Becher manuscript book. There are many text variations dated before and after the arrival of the Pūhoi settlers in 1863. As the content of the folk song *A Dampferl im Kopf* (*A little steamer in the head*) is comparable to the farmer's life, the words from that song have been selected and translated by Ralf Heimrath (2020) into the Egerlander dialect for our song version. Metaphorically, the meaning could be seen as a large group of people dancing around like a swarm of bees in the sky.

SOURCES *Text:* From Kremser, *Wiener Lieder und Tänze* (1912). *Music:* Charles Becher manuscript book. See also p. 158.

Singing at the Pūhoi pub c. 1970, with a traditional group of violin, dudelsack and button accordian. *PHS 0071*

9.
Music for dancing

Eins und zwei und drei und vier

One and two and three and four

Medley: Sprat polka (Krebs-Polka)

Literal translations from Deitsch

English

One and two and three and four,
you chubby lady could go with me,
and come and dance with me.

High German

Eins und zwei und drei und vier,
du mollige Frau könntest mit mir gehn,
und komm und tanz mit mir.

Notes

This piece is popular in Pūhoi as a dance, the *Sprat polka*. The dancers sing a chorus and then break out into dance. The first line is so obvious that nowadays one hears it in German rather than the Pūhoi dialect, but a word like *mållega* brings it back to the old dialect. In Germany, it is a common folk dance known as *Krebspolka, Krebs-Polka* or *Manchester* in which the dancers have to move backwards like a crab (hence the title *Krebs*). These tunes are also used for a Czech song about buying corduroy to make a vest. Hence the title 'Manchester', where the corduroy was made. Sprat derives from the Czech *zpět*, meaning to go backwards.

SOURCES *Text:* From Judith Williams. *Music:* Charles Becher manuscript book; Baumann (1985). See also p. 157.

Oins, zwoi, drei, väir, fimf, sechs, siem

One, two, three, four, five, six, seven

Prince of Wales Schottischer

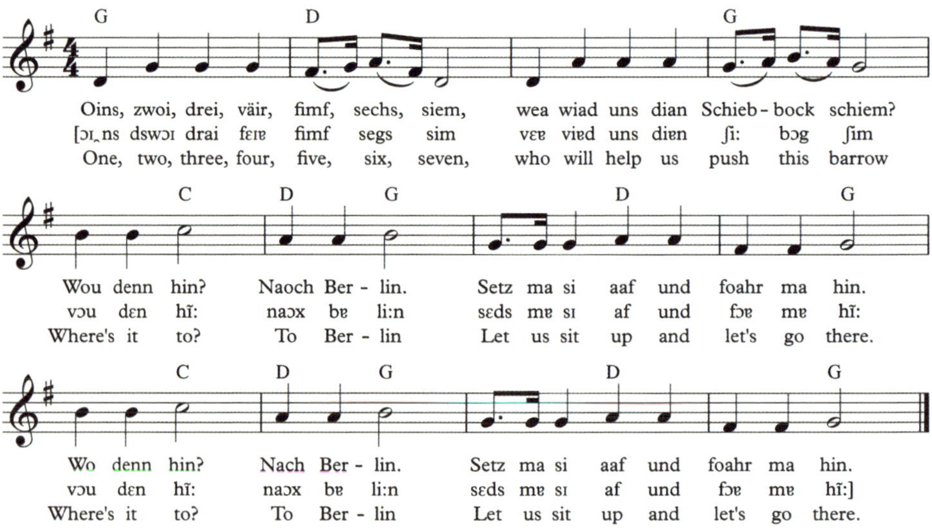

Literal translations from Deitsch

English

One, two, three, four, five, six, seven,
who will help us push the barrow?
Where to? To Berlin.
Let's sit up and let's go there.

High German

Eins, zwei, drei, vier, fünf, sechs, sieben,
wer wird uns den Schubkarren schieben?
Wo denn hin? Nach Berlin.
Setzen wir uns auf und fahren wir hin.

Notes

The melody of this popular song is very similar to *Gsundhait mainer und Gsundhait dainer* (p. 78) and follows a popular tradition of hearty, humorous songs that can be used for dancing and, of course, drinking.

The text is identical to the children's folksong and dance *Siebenschritt* (*Seven steps*). As a children's song, there is no special reason or context for the use of Berlin as the destination. Berlin became the German capital in 1871 but before that the city was the capital of Prussia, a land in the north, far from Bohemia. There are two likely reasons that Berlin is named in the song: it works with the rhyme and it was an unknown and faraway city, a place of fantasy.

Prince of Wales Schottischer

Instrumental version

SOURCES *Text:* From Judith Williams. *Music:* Charles Becher manuscript book. *Instrumental version music:* Baumann (1985). See also p. 158.

Moidl rupf di, zupf di, kämm di schäi(n)

Darling primp and pluck and comb yourself

Literal translations from Deitsch

English	*High German*
Girl, primp yourself, pluck yourself, comb yourself well,	Mädchen rupf dich, zupf dich, kämm dich schön,
on Saturday we're going to the wedding.	am Samstag werden wir auf die Hochzeit gehen.
Let's put on pretty little shoes and stockings,	Legen wir schöne Schühlein und Strümpflein an,
so that we can dance right well.	dass man recht schön tanzen kann.

Notes

This is another song recorded by Werner Droescher in 1963, but the melody is not too clear on the recording. However, the Becher manuscript provided the tune of the song together with the instrumental section. A similar version of the song is also known in the Oberfranken region, neighbouring northern Egerland.

SOURCES *Text and music:* From the recording by Werner Droescher (1963), transcribed by Ralf Heimrath and Roger Buckton. *Music:* Charles Becher manuscript book. *Informants:* Alice and Anton Bayer, Judith Williams collection. See also p. 160.

Dancing the Egerland dance, *Af Matzlbooch*, at the 150th anniversary of the Bohemians settling at Ōhaupō in 2014. *PHS 3734*

Umandum – Ländler (1)

Umandum – Ländler (2)

Notes

These two ländlers[12] provide the music for a traditional 19th-century dance, the umandum. Collected from Laurie Rauner by Erich Baumann during a visit to Pūhoi in 1984, they were published in Baumann's collection, *Alt-Egerländer Tänze*. Baumann references them as also being played in the regions of Mies (Stříbro), Staab (Stod) and Pilsen.

The two dances next appeared in New Zealand in 1993 as the opening numbers on the Puhoi Band's CD *Die Booei Musikgruppe*. In the CD notes they are described as waltzes, another example of old tunes being adapted to the newer styles of dancing the Egerlanders would have encountered in New Zealand. Musically the result is an increase in tempo, for the ländler is slower than the waltz.

The titles of the tunes are given as *Dudelsack waltz* and *Food waltz*. Roger Buckton, producer of the CD, remembers that at the time of the recording, tunes were being recalled but not always titles, so for the sake of the recording, some were created on the spot.

Ländler (1) with a violin is well suited to the dudelsack and this could be the reason for the title, but it is not known why Ländler (2) should be linked to food. Its first melody (bars 1–16) is the well-known German folk song *Du, du liegst mir in Herzen* (*You are in my heart*). There is also a version in Brosch (1997), *Du bist in mein Gart'n eingstiegn* (no. 2282), in which one of the singers was a Gustav Bayer. Even though Laurie Rauner was the source for both the Egerland and Pūhoi versions, there is a significant variation in the music for Ländler (1). Both dances shown here are transcribed from the Pūhoi CD. The transcription and second part were done by Roger Buckton.

SOURCES *Music:* Baumann (1985). *Recording: Die Booei Musikgruppe: Bohemian Music from Pūhoi* (1993).

| *Finger Polka* at the Pūhoi Market in April 2014. *PHS 3943*

Finger polka

Notes

No collection of Pūhoi dance music would be complete without *Finger polka*. It is the Pūhoi dance which almost everyone knows and is as popular for adults as it is with children. Although it is considered a unique Pūhoi dance, other versions of the same dance can be found in many areas of Europe. The polka itself dates back to a Czech peasant dance in Bohemia. Introduced to Prague ballrooms in 1835, it quickly became the rage of 19th-century Europe and America. Finger wagging as a dance action dates back at least to Thoinot Arbeau (1519–1595). This French priest's dancing book, *Orchesography* (1589), includes such a dance, the *Branle des Lavandières* (Washerwomen's Branle).

SOURCES *Recording:* Puhoi Band (1993), transcription and arrangement by Roger Buckton. *Music:* Thoinot Arbeau, *Orchesography* (1589). See also p. 160.

PART TWO

Pūhoi's cultural heritage

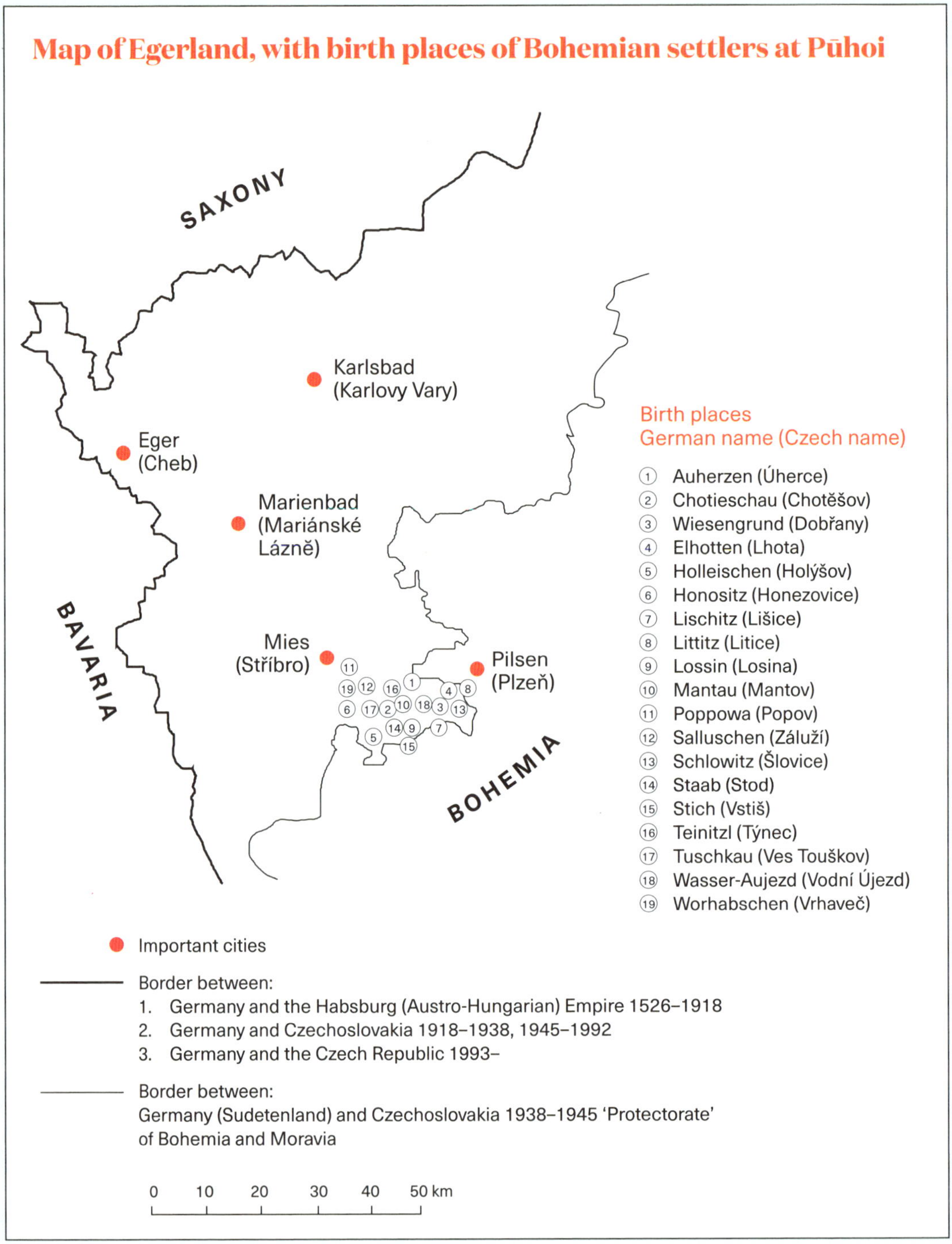

Birthplaces of the immigrants from northwest Bohemian (Egerland) to New Zealand, 1860–1876. *From Heller, 2005*

10.
The origins of the music

Although the settlers at Pūhoi came from the historic country of Bohemia (a kingdom in the Holy Roman Empire and subsequently a province in the Habsburg (Austrian) Empire), with Prague as its capital, their language was based on the historical region of Egerland (in the far northwest of Bohemia). They did not speak High German but rather a dialect they called Deitsch. Werner Droescher identified Deitsch as North Bavarian and the map opposite indicates the Egerlander dialect's linguistic region as a sub-area within North Bavaria.[13] Just as a Geordie accent will reveal that a person comes from Newcastle in the northeast of England, so Deitsch can place people as being from an area around Staab, near Pilsen. Many of the settlers came from the neighbouring town of Chotieschau, now Chotěšov. The accompanying map shows the area of the Egerlander dialect as being between the borders of Bavaria, Saxony and Bohemia.

The songs reproduced in this book are first in Deitsch, with a phonetic guide to pronunciation, and then English (accompanied by literal translations of the Deitsch in English and High German). Many have an archaic quality as they are not songs from the late 19th century when the Pūhoi settlers arrived, but rather from much earlier times. They had already been passed down through many generations before immigration to New Zealand. *Der wos döi bayrisch Duadl will hom* (*Who wants Bavarian Dora must have*, p. 48) with its changing metre of two and three beats is a traditional dance that was first copied by Thomas Kunz in 1825 from the Gubernial Collection in Bohemia.[14] It was collected as part of a capturing of traditional folk music of the region so it can be assumed that it had already been sung and danced to by several generations.

Bearing in mind the age of these songs, they can give clues to what life was like in the region the Pūhoi migrants came from. Unlike England, which was the first country to industrialise, economic and social change was slower in central Europe. However, even the Habsburg (Austro-Hungarian) Empire, which controlled the deeply conservative and rural region of Bohemia, was affected by revolution in 1848. Bohemia itself experienced armed conflict during the Prague uprising of that same year. The Habsburg Empire prevailed and successfully regained control and centralised during this time, with Vienna becoming the official centre of power. The middle of the 19th century was a very unsettled period in Europe, which may have been the driver of much of the emigration at that time, especially if conscription was a likelihood.

But all this was perhaps far removed from the subjects of the traditional songs. They describe village life with its traditions, customs and folklore as well as the influence of the Roman Catholic Church. For many, time was measured by the annual calendar that moved from one anniversary or feast day to the next, usually tied to the church year and frequently related to agricultural practices. For example, Salzmann and Scheufler noted that fields were to be ploughed by Saint Gregory's Day (12 March), cabbages and turnips were to be sown on Saint Mark the Evangelist's Day (25 April) and transplanted on Saint Vitus's Day (15 June).[15] Another important day was associated with Easter (see Maia custom on p. 68).

Arrival in Pūhoi would have been a huge shock to these settlers but they came and developed the land as a society bonded by their language, their Roman Catholic faith and generations of communal and traditional folklore practices.

The land they settled had been sold to the government by Te Hemara Tauhia, leader of Te Kawerau/Ngāti Rongo hapū of Ngāti Whātua, and it was his people who built the first shelters for the new arrivals and helped them with food during the lean early years. The relationship between the two groups was generally cordial and in 1872 the *Auckland Weekly News* describes a 'Great Native Festival at Puhoi':

> Maori and pakeha had assembled, and seemed resolved to make the most of an enjoyable day. Te Hemera, the host of the occasion, and his kindly disposed and amiable wife, Miriam, did their utmost to make those who had accepted their invitation feel themselves truly welcome; and hospitality to its greatest extent was bestowed on one and all. A dinner was served, the entire preparation having been performed by natives in their own 'kapa maori', the cookery whereof was all a gourmand could desire . . .[16]

Reporters were equally interested in the 'exotic' culture of the Bohemians. In 1866, only three years after their arrival, a reporter for the *Daily Southern Cross* wrote:

> The cottages and clearings are scattered along the banks of the creek . . . It is essentially a 'poor man's' settlement but nevertheless prosperous and sound, politically.
>
> On Sundays and holidays [i.e. anniversary days] the inhabitants, who are chiefly from Bohemia and South Germany, put on their German habiliments, and while listening to their Teutonic dialects, and viewing their characteristic costumes, one might fancy oneself again in Schwar[t]zwald, or amongst the mountains of Carinthia.[17]

That same year, Captain Martin Krippner (1817–1894, see p. 104) enlisted all the single men of Pūhoi and five of the married men to join his 3rd Waikato Regiment (made up of European settlers based in and around Cambridge) to fight in the New Zealand Wars in Waikato. Happily, they were never actually in combat but as a result each received 50 to 60 acres of land and so founded a second Bohemian settlement at Ōhaupō, near Hamilton.

The enigmatic Captain Krippner (born in Mantau, Bohemia) is credited with being the person who organised the Pūhoi settlement and encouraged his fellow countrymen to immigrate to New Zealand. Krippner arrived in New Zealand in 1860 with his English wife, Emily Longdill, and their children and a few other families, including his brother Johannes (Hans).

Emily began teaching the Pūhoi children in 1863. The children were taught using their dialect, Deitsch. However, recognising that the language of the future in New Zealand was English, from 1884 lessons were taught exclusively in English,

Captain Martin Krippner

Captain Krippner is a controversial character. Described by various sources as entrepreneurial, educated, a family man, courageous, foolhardy, a social climber, an adventurist or an opportunist, he was certainly a man of natural ability and personal charm. Pūhoi as a Bohemian settlement would not have come into being without him. His wife, Emily Krippner (née Longdill), was an Englishwoman, and the two met in Frankfurt, where Emily was living with her sister after the death of their parents.

Encouraged by Emily's brother, Pynson Wilmot Longdill, Emily and Martin, their three sons, daughter and niece, immigrated to Auckland in 1860. Krippner quickly became well known in government and military circles and he was granted permission to organise a settlement of Bohemian people at Pūhoi with the promise of a 40-acre grant for each adult immigrant and a 20-acre grant for each child over five years of age. The scheme was very attractive to the Bohemian pioneers, who had no chance of owning their own land; about 30 families took up the offer, arriving in 1863.

As with many who promoted settlement in New Zealand, Captain Krippner was later criticised for bringing the Bohemians to the steep, isolated, bush-clad hills of Pūhoi; he had greatly exaggerated the quality of the land.

To help provide income for the new settlers, and because he and his wife were possibly the only English speakers, it was Krippner who arranged markets for the firewood, shingles, fenceposts, fungus, tanekaha bark (used in the tanning industry) and charcoal gleaned from the bush. He arranged for the river to be cleared of snags to enable ships to transport the produce from Pūhoi.

By the 1880s Pūhoi was beginning to find its feet and with a well-established economy and familiarity with the English language, they no longer needed the Krippners to act as intermediaries between them and wider society. There was some criticism of Krippner's actions over the previous 20 years, but their contribution to the settlement was also acknowledged, and the settlers moved the couple to a home they'd built for them in Pulham Road, Warkworth.

Jenny Schollum

Captain Martin Krippner, 3rd Regiment, Waikato Militia (German Legion), in full military uniform, c. 1900. *William Francis Robert Gordon, collection of Puke Ariki, New Plymouth*

HOW WE HAVE GROWN.
PUHOI ANNIVERSARY
1863-1913

and Deitsch became the vernacular language spoken at home and in the bush.

Until the beginning of the First World War (1914–1918), the villagers usually communicated in dialect. Following the outbreak of war, German was the language of the enemy and it was advantageous to speak English in public. Dialect thus retreated further into the domestic realm. With improvements in transport and infrastructure, dialect-speaking inhabitants began moving away from Pūhoi. There was also an influx of non-German-speaking people into the area, with more mixed marriages as a result. These changes meant that the use of the dialect was further reduced and English became the main language of the Pūhoi community.

From the 1930s onwards, fewer and fewer people in Pūhoi spoke Deitsch. Then came the Second World War (1939–1945) and it was once again prudent to hide one's German roots.

At the 1963 centennial celebrations of the first Bohemian arrivals at Pūhoi, Werner Droescher recorded the old settlers singing some of their traditional songs, but by 1969, he commented:

> . . . things have changed . . . Life has become quieter. The once typical Egerländer festivities have now given way to a typical New Zealand life: agricultural shows, cricket and rugby matches. Only for the annual jubilee [held on 29 June] many of the relations come back to their old home and the old dances are once again danced by the elderly folk.[18]

Opposite above: Pūhoi's 50th anniversary. *PHS 0976*

Opposite below: Crowds celebrating the 1963 re-enactment of the 1863 landings at Pūhoi. *PHS 0192*

Ōhaupō: 'The Place Where the Wind Blows at Night'

Ōhaupō, a small rural settlement, lies on State Highway 3, 17 kilometres south of Hamilton. The main highway was once an important Māori trail between Kirikiriroa Hamilton and Otawhao Te Awamutu.

Captain Martin Krippner commanded a company that was part of the 3rd Regiment of the Waikato Militia and in 1864 he conscripted some of Pūhoi's most able young men, at a time when the settlers were fighting for survival in the dense bush. It is ironic that a reason for these young men leaving Bohemia had been to avoid conscription in the Imperial Austrian Army. One of the men who enlisted was Joseph Paul, the original dudelsack player of Pūhoi. However, he was discharged on account of 'lack of strength' and returned to Pūhoi.

After the war, and without having seen any actual fighting, all the men were rewarded with confiscated Māori land at Ōhaupō, and so founded a second Bohemian settlement. Wives and families from Pūhoi joined their men, including Michael and Barbara Krippner and family, Hans and Elizabeth Krippner, Joseph and Anna Karl and family, Anton and Barbara Turnwald.

Anton Turnwald established a butchery and the Karls planted a cherry orchard and kept bees. Henry Gleye, a carpenter who married Catherine Turnwald, built many of the first homes in the settlement. Michael Krippner was the proud possessor of the first cow. The families of Joseph and Margaret Sittauer and Joseph and Anna Papesch and Wenzl and Anna Karl joined them in 1876 and 1884 respectively.

Traditional Bohemian music has been strong in the Waikato and is thought to have been taken there by Annie Wech, who had married George Krippner, a grandson of Michael and Barbara Krippner, in 1928. The Ōhaupō members of the Krippner family have been much appreciated as musicians for the community and have returned to Pūhoi to provide a band for many occasions.

Above: Celebrations for the 150th anniversary of the settlement of the Pūhoi Bohemians at Ōhaupō in 2014. *PHS 3720*

Opposite: Anton Turnwald was one of the original settlers to move from Pūhoi to Ōhaupō. *Te Awamutu Museum Collection PH1051*

11.
The importance of singing and dancing

Dancing in the Pūhoi hall was popular for many years and the musicians of Pūhoi were expected to play the latest colonial dances such as the waltz and the polka. By linking several of the old songs, a medley could be compiled of sufficient length for the duration of these dances. Two examples in this book are the instrumental dance medleys *Summer air in May waltz* (p. 28) and *Schedewy polka* (p. 30). No doubt these more traditional sources for dancing were popular because the dancers would have remembered the tunes and words of the old Bohemian songs.

The use of song melodies for dancing illustrates the popularity of this activity. Father Silk, their parish priest, wrote that, 'Dancing has unfortunately come to stay, not only in Pūhoi but also wherever a few individuals can be gathered together.'[11]

Dancing in the hall was complemented by dancing in the home, an old Bohemian custom. If there was no instrumentalist available, they could dance to their own singing (surely another reason why these songs have survived for so long). This collection, therefore, contains some dance music, and where song texts are known, these have been included.

The Pūhoi settlers were noted for their love of dancing at the time and there are many accounts of dancing in the early years.

| A postcard showing dancing in Staab, Bohemia c. 1890. *Michael Cwach Collection*

> I have witnessed dancing in many countries — the cross-road break-down, Ireland; the Highland fling, Ayreshire; the Spanish fandango, Mexico; but nowhere have I seen dancing so thoroughly gone into so heartily as in Pūhoi. All ages from 7 to 70 assemble in the dance-room, and as long as the fiddler is able to wield the bow or the piper squeeze out a note, so long do they tread to the measure of the Reichstachel [Reichsapfel], Dumadum [Umadum], etc. It is no uncommon thing to have dancing continued unceasingly night after night for a week . . .[19]

Forgiving a colonial reporter for misspelling the names of the dances, it can be seen how traditional Bohemian dances using the old tunes and songs continued in Pūhoi throughout the rest of the 19th century.

New generations then wanted the latest dances — the polka and waltz being especially popular. The old dances were still enjoyed for particular occasions, such as the anniversary day of the Bohemian settlement at Pūhoi (29 June), weddings, and perhaps a special birthday of one of the ageing settlers, but it was the new dances that were now popular.

The Bohemian flair for music ensured that most dances employed the services of Bohemian musicians. These musicians looked to the traditional songs that they knew and joined songs of similar tempo and metre together to create medleys suitable for the new dances.

By the late 20th century, some of the third-generation Bohemians would still have recalled the words, perhaps singing along with the band — just in time to be recorded by Werner Droescher and others in the 1960s. Today, dances in the Puhoi Hall featuring the traditional dances are infrequent, but Bohemian dance groups, including those for children, continue to keep the traditional Egerlander dances alive.

Dancing in the Pūhoi hall in celebration of the 150th anniversary of the arrival of the ship *Liverpool* in 1866. The dancers' costumes illustrate some of the local characteristics of their particular districts. Three women in the front are wearing Chotieschau costumes notable for the red stockings. The dancer on the left with white stockings is wearing a pastel-blue skirt with black lace, typical of Bischofteinitz. The men are wearing black trousers, which is the norm for almost the whole of Egerland; only in Chotieschau and its surroundings did the men wear yellow trousers and blue coats, showing the influence of nearby Czech culture (see p. 115). *PHS 4464*

BOHEMIAN
ASSOCIATION NZ

Pūhoi/Ōhaupō costumes (Die Tracht)

There are nine cultural districts in the Egerland area and each district has its own costume (known as tracht). The Bohemian settlers at Pūhoi came from Chotieschau and its neighbouring districts of Mies to the north and Bischofteinitz to the south. The costumes worn by both men and women serve as a visual statement of a person's heritage and kinship. Within the Egerland region there were a number of relatively small districts, each of which had developed its own unique cultural identity as reflected in its dialect, songs and dances, food and drink and clothes.

Above: In the yard of No. 9 Tuschbau village near Staab, not far from Chotieschau. It is interesting to see the woman at the well wearing Die Tracht, but water is needed even on Sundays, or perhaps it was for the camera. The wide floral band material just above the hemline is characteristic of the Chotieschau style. *From Hofmann*

Opposite: Folk costume of the Chotieschau–Kladrau region around 1830–1860 after a watercolour by Gustav Zindel. Note the narrow pleats of the women's skirts, while the men's boots and trousers reflect a Czech influence. *From Hofmann*

For most people, their village or town was their world. Communication with the 'outside world' was typically by word of mouth, and transportation was by foot, or horse and cart for the more affluent. Horse-drawn train carriages had started in the region in 1828 and by 1863 the Pūhoi settlers travelled by steam train to Prague and thence to the port of Hamburg in Germany. This was a time when the impact of the railways was only beginning to be asserted in Europe so the way of life and customs were still influenced by the traditions of centuries of serfdom.

Within the administrative district of Pilsen, the small town of Chotieschau (Czech: Chotěšov) was the home of a majority of the settlers, and their costumes reflect the stylistic characteristics of that region. Chotieschau costumes also demonstrate the strong influence of neighbouring Czech regions, such as the red stockings worn by the women.

Since the 19th century, the design of costumes has changed from the more elaborate to something more practical for present-day travel and dancing. In Pūhoi and Ōhaupō the dance groups have been the pioneers of the restoration of the custom of wearing Die Tracht. But as in Germany and Austria, New Zealand Bohemians are beginning to favour wearing their tracht for special occasions such as at the funeral of noted Ōhaupō resident Christine Krippner in 2024.

Opposite: The parents of Dora Schollum, photographed in Pilsen, date unknown. The striped apron is a characteristic of a Chotieschau costume. *Schollum family album, PHS 1277*

12. The dialect of Pūhoi's settlers

When we hear someone speak in a way that is different to ourselves, we might think of where that person is from; Scotland, North America or a region within a country, such as the north of England. In other words, she or he speaks with an 'accent'. An accent can also denote social class. While we all speak the 'King's English', to a New Zealander, King Charles himself speaks with an accent that is recognisable as an English person from the upper classes. Happily in English there is no change in spelling across the wide range of accents we hear, unless the sounds of a particular accent are required for a special situation, such as in a play or film. The words are spelled the same way regardless of how they are pronounced.

German is written more phonetically than English. What you see is what you say, and what you hear is what you write. There are no silent letters and no various possibilities for pronunciation as with 'ough' (enough, ought, cough, though) in English. The spelling of each word is strongly indicative of the pronunciation and if there is any variation, a letter may have an umlaut to indicate a change of sound, as in *die Mädchen* (the girls). So in singing the text of a new song, whether it is in Deitsch or High German, the spelling is always a helpful guide as to how to pronounce the language reasonably accurately.

As a dialect of German, the written words of Deitsch reflect this process. The spelling gives clues to the pronunciation of the dialect because the people of Egerland spoke their language in a different way to other parts of Germany.

The phonetic symbols also seen in the songs take this process a step further because a phonetic character or group of characters precisely provides the pronunciation required.

The following tables give English speakers a guide to the pronunciation of Deitsch and German words through the spelling of a word, and for additional accuracy the phonetic alphabet has been provided. Note that the phonetics have been shown for all the songs.

Deitsch, also known as the Staab dialect, belongs to the North Bavarian sub-dialect of Austro-Bavarian, which again can be subdivided into Core-Egerland (Kernegerland), South-Egerland and finally the Staab Dialect (Deitsch).

Inevitably, Deitsch has ceased to be the native language of Pūhoi's inhabitants. It is a relic of a bygone era but has been preserved in different ways; in collections of old songs, in poetic writings, or as audio recordings of spoken texts. Metaphorically, the Deitsch language island of Pūhoi has sunk beneath the waves of the English language. Occasionally, some elements are fished out of the water and brought to light. These dialect songs can be seen as linguistic and musical treasures that have been raised from the deep.

Pronunciation guide for English speakers

Character	Phonetic symbol	Explanations, examples in Deitsch	Compare with English
a	[a]	shortly pronounced	u in English run, sun, cut
a, aa	[a:]	long pronounced	the 1st syllable of English rather
a	[ɐ]	without accent	e in the 2nd syllable of after
å	[ɔ]	Håns, Måidl	a in English all, wall, small, call
ä	[ɛ]	väia	1st syllable in mention
ai	[ai]	ai(n), Wai (Weib)	wife, bite, night
ao, au	[aɔ]	Bauer	like ow or ou in English cow, loud, now
e	[ɛ]	Hemd	1st syllable in terror
e	[e]	wer, der	(to) wear (a cloth)
ei, äi	[ɛi]	gäih, schäi(n)	wait, late
i	[i]	shortly pronounced	bit, kiss, dig
i, ie, ih	[i:]	long pronounced	keep, beat, deep
(n)		give a nasal quality to the previous vowel	no equivalence in English
o	[ɔ]	open pronounced	often, long, God, dollar
o	[o]	closed pronounced	more, old, Mozart
ö	[ø]	Göld	shirt, word, dirty, church, girl
ou	[ou]	Bou	show, blow, know
r		like an Italian ‘r’ with a fluttering tongue	similar to Scottish rolled ‘r’
sch	[ʃ]	schäi(n)	English sh
u	[u]	shortly pronounced	push, put
u, uh	[u:]	long pronounced	loose, goose
ü	[y]	müssen	Ypsilon

v	[f]	in a word with Germanic roots like a ‘f’	German vier = English four
v	[v]	in a loanword from another language	German Violine = English violin
y	[y]	a bit darker than e	Ypsilon

The following examples from the songs illustrate some of these points:

Example 1:
Baua heng dai(n) Bumml ua(n) (p. 34)

Deitsch

Baua heng dai(n) Bumml ua(n), dass a mi niat stoussn kua(n).
Stasst a mi, sou straof i di, hunnad Dollar kost a di.
Hunnad Dollar is in Göld, dao glaa mi oina, wos mi gföld,
dass mi rupfd und dass mi zupfd und dass mit mi ins Bett ai(n) hupfd.

High German

Bauer, häng dein’ Bummel an, dass er mich nicht stoßen kann.
Stößt er mich, so straf’ ich dich. Hundert Dollar kost’ er dich.
Hundert Dollar ist ein Geld, da glaub’ mir einer, was mir g’fällt,
dass (er) mich rupft und dass (er) mich zupft und dass (er) mit mir ins Bett hinein hüpft.

English

Farmer, tie up your bull, so that he can’t butt me.
If he butts me, I’ll punish you. A hundred dollars it will cost you.
A hundred dollars is a lot of money, believe me what I would like is
that he [the bull] plucks and picks me and hops into bed with me.

The Deitsch dialect can be identified in the pronunciation of the following words (phonetics shown in square parenthesis):

Deitsch	High German	English
(er) kua(n) [kuã]	(er) kann [kan]	(he) can
niat [nĩɐ'd]	nicht [nixd]	not
stoussn [ʃdousn]	stoßen [ʃdo:sn]	push
Göld [gø:ld]	Geld [gɛld]	money
oina [oinɐ] / uina [uinɐ]	einer [ainɐ]	(some)one

A particularly significant characteristic of the dialect is the so-called 'tipped' diphthong. This has its origins in Middle High German language (MHG) c. 1200 (medieval German, see Lexer/Pretzel 1999 on Middle High German vocabulary). For instance, the long vowel *u* [u:] found in many of today's words often originates from MHG *uo*. Deitsch turns *uo* into *ou*.

Deitsch	Middle High German	Modern High German	English
gout [goud]	guot [guot]	gut [gu:t]	good
Fouß [fous]	fuoz [fuos]	Fuß [fu:s]	foot
Roubm [roum]	ruobe [ruobə]	Rübe [ry:bə]	turnip
Bou [bou]	buobe [buobə]	Bub [bub] (Junge, Knabe)	boy
Boum [boum]	buoben [buɐm]	Buben [bu:bən]	boys

The long vowel *ie/ih/i* [i:] spoken today mostly originates from MHG *ie* [iə]. In middle Bavarian, this is an *ia* [iɐ], and in North Bavarian Deitsch, this is an *äi* [ɛɪ] or *öi* [øɪ].

Deitsch	High German	English
däi [dɛɪ] / döi [døɪ]	die [di:]	they
wäi [vɛɪ] / wöi [vøɪ]	wie [vi:]	how
Bäia/Böia [bɛiɐ]	Bier [bi:ɐ]	beer
läiwa [lɛivɐ]	lieber [li:bɐ]	rather
väia [fɛiɐ]	vier [fi:ɐ]	four

Example 2:
Dra Åckarla Kraat (p. 50)

The Deitsch pronunciation of *wie* (how), *die* (they), *lieber* (rather), *Rüben* (turnips) and *Buben* (boys) is illustrated in this song.

Deitsch

Dra Åckarla Kraat, draa Åckarla Roum,
wöi schänna döi Måi(d)la, wöi löiwa hooms Boum.

High German

Drei Äckerlein Kraut, drei Äckerlein Rüben,
je schöner die Mädchen, desto lieben haben sie Buben.

English

Three small fields with cabbage, three small fields with turnips,
The prettier the girls, the more liked by the boys.

Example 3:
The numeral vier [fiːɐ] (four) is in Deitsch väia

Deitsch

Oins, zwoi, drai, väia, fimf, sechs, siem . . .
[oins dsvoi drai fɛiɐ fimf segs siːm]

High German

Eins, zwei, drei, vier, fünf, sechs, sieben . . .
[ains dsvai drai fiːɐ fynf segs siːbən]

English

One, two, three, four, five, six, seven . . .

13.
Culture bearers: Our informants and their families

The first Bohemian immigrants arrived at Pūhoi in the year 1863 and anniversaries of this event have been celebrated ever since. Of all the celebrations, the centennial in 1963 must have been one of the most memorable.

Although all the original settlers had long since departed this earth, many attending the 100th anniversary recalled with affection and heart-felt memories, happy family times sharing dialect songs and sayings from their grandparents. Indeed, a number of songs in this collection were located on recordings from community singing in the Puhoi Hall and other places in 1963. At that time, many of the informants were on the senior side of 50 years.

With exceptions, those of the fourth generation, who were under 50 years old in 1963, did not know the songs so it is fortunate that between approximately 1960 and 1990, the song memories of their grandparents were captured. Pūhoi historian Jenny Schollum noted that the generation born in the 1940s could sing bits of the songs but did not necessarily understand the meaning of the text.

Two family tree diagrams are provided in this section (pp. 132, 142) and given the tangle of family relationships in the small community, it may be helpful to refer to these when reading the following section.

From left: Laurie Rauner and Jim Rauner (partly obscured) on accordions; Philip Wech playing the dudelsack and Ben Bayer on violin at the 1963 centennial of the first Bohemians arriving at Pūhoi. *PHS 0202*

The Rauner–Bayer families

Robert (Bob) Wech (1892–1978) was our oldest informant. Bob's father Matthew (1863–1920) was born at Lossin 34, Bohemia (Lossin was a small village where the houses were numbered) and arrived as a three-year-old with his parents on the ship *Liverpool* in 1866. Matthew's wife Anna (Hendl) (1868–1948), Bob's mother, was born at Lossin 7, and arrived in Pūhoi in 1875. The Hendl family (known as Hennl then) lived near to the Rauners at Lossin 8. Young Bob Wech would have spoken Deitsch at home, while English was spoken at the school by the time he attended in the late 1890s.

Bob's wife Christina spoke Deitsch at home for the first 10 years of her life, 1899–1909. At school, she learned English and by the early 1900s speaking the 'dialect' at school was not allowed. Communication at home was in Deitsch as her father, John Bayer (1871–1948), and mother, Elizabeth (née Rauner) (1872–1952), were born at Pūhoi at a time when Deitsch would have been the dominant vernacular language there. They were both children of parents born in Bohemia

Above: Christina (née Bayer) and Bob Wech at their golden wedding celebrations in 1969. *PHS 4250*

Opposite: Joe Tolhopf playing the old Pūhoi dudelsack on stage during the visit of the Egerlanders in 1984. *PHS 0391*

whose native language was Deitsch. John and Elizabeth learned English at school but to them it was as a foreign language.

John and Elizabeth Bayer had a family of eight children including Christina. One brother, Ben (1905–1997), played the violin and another, Anton (Tony) (1913–2010), had a reputation for narrating some of the more colourful dialect rhymes and jokes. Anton married Alice Tolhopf (1914–2003), making the link with another important musical family, the Tolhopfs. Joe Tolhopf (1928–2004) was born when his father Joseph Tolhopf was 47 years of age. So, in effect, Joe jumped a generation and could remember songs and stories from an earlier time compared with many of his peers.

In the Puhoi Band, Ben Bayer was valued for remembering the old tunes and songs. Another sibling, Annie (1901–1999), played the violin. She married dudelsack and accordion player Jim Rauner (1900–1978). Maureen Roase wrote that Annie's memory 'for the traditional folk songs of her childhood never faltered and in her nineties neither did her rhythm'.[20] It was Annie who sang *Nao an Winta kinnt da Summa* (After Winter Comes the Summer) to be recorded by her niece, Dot Berger (Wech) (1928–2003). Dot's brother Philip Wech (1926–1997) was the dudelsack player in the band for many years until his death in 1997. Dot and Philip

BAND

Above: The location of the home of the Rauners, Lossin 8, Bohemia, 2023. Lossin was also home to the Wechs and Hennl (Hennls). *Michael Cwach*

Below: Johann and Annie Rauner, c. 1900s. *PHS 3491*

did not learn the dialect and a glance at the family tree suggests a reason: they were fourth-generation Bohemians whereas the others were only third-generation.

While we acknowledge the assistance of Christina, Ben, Anton (Tony) and Annie with gratitude, we record that it was their parents, John and Elizabeth Bayer, living in Tahekeroa (further inland from Pūhoi) who provided a foundation of music, dialect and love of the Bohemian culture as part of their family nurturing.

Maureen Roase wrote about this family:

> Typical pioneer life did nothing to quell the musical instinct that ran through their veins and despite anything except the bare essentials survival was a struggle. Family strength was bound by their music. Elizabeth played the accordion and the children were brought up with as much music or more, than bread on the table.[21]

Johann Rauner (1844–1913) was born at Lossin 8 and came to New Zealand in 1863 on the *War Spirit* at the age of 19. In 1870 he married Annie Paul (1853–1919), who had also been on the *War Spirit*. Annie was the daughter of Joseph Paul (1816–1910, see photo p. 141), the person who introduced to Pūhoi and played that unique musical instrument the dudelsack. (The Paul family had lived at the village of Poppowa, house number 9.)

When they married in 1870, Johann (26) and Annie (17) would have known little English. Their language was Deitsch. Bohemians have a reputation for large families, and between 1872 and 1892, Annie produced 17 children, all of whom experienced a home in which Deitsch was their language of communication. Two of these children have already been mentioned: Elizabeth, who married John Bayer, and James (Jim), who married Annie Bayer.

Another child, Anton (1876–1944), married Elizabeth Wech (1890–1971) in 1912 and they had six children including Lawrence (Laurie) (1920–2006) and Fred (1928–2022). Laurie was the leader of the Puhoi Band and highly respected for his knowledge and memory of the repertoire. Fred was also a good and loyal member of the band, but is now remembered as probably the last person to be able to speak the Pūhoi dialect. Laurie spoke the dialect fluently and knew many songs but he seemed to prefer playing them to singing. Fred also didn't seem to sing much, but he did have a good, accurate voice and in an interview in 2017 he readily sang the songs that he remembered.

So Johann and Annie (née Paul) Rauner and Wenzl (1938–1887) and Anna (née Wenzlick) (1842–1911) Bayer are the grandparents and great-grandparents (either directly or through marriage) of a majority of the informants in this study. Their enthusiasm and talent for music, expressed through singing the dialect songs, and playing the accordion, violin and dudelsack, was responsible for a major part of the Pūhoi music tradition.

For the very first pioneers arriving in 1863, in particular, there must have been considerable cultural distress and disbelief on seeing their new home.[22] Hard-pressed to eat and survive while breaking in the New Zealand bush, they were also faced with a change in climate and seasons; the need to learn English to communicate with the few other people in the area and to establish trade with wider Auckland; and the absence of a sizeable community to support their traditions and folklore.

All of these challenges could have contributed to a significant decline in singing the old songs and the interest in learning traditional songs and games by their children. However, singing these traditional songs in their homes, at the pub and in the hall also provided some degree of comfort and cultural continuity. Unlike much of the rest of colonial New Zealand, where settlers came from widely separated geographical regions, such as those from across the British Isles, these settlers were from a relatively small, regional part of Europe with a distinct common heritage. In New Zealand, isolated by geography and language, their songs and dances provided a sense of social cohesion as they coped with the challenges of basic survival.

Nor should we forget the part played by the church. As devout Roman Catholics, the coming together for worship through prayer and praise were all part of the strong bonds that have remained to this day. In 2023, Gerard Straka commented that Sunday Mass, in addition to its religious significance, was an important social occasion:

> I remember in the 1960s and '70s after Mass, families would talk for ages (seemed like hours!) outside the church. That would have been even truer in the early days given the long walks many families had just to get to Mass. My grandmother, Margaret, remembered many families would come down to the Puhoi Hotel for lunch.[23]

Wenzl and Anna (née Wenzlick) Bayer and family, c. 1870s. *PHS 5031*

Informants from the Rauner–Bayer family tree (siblings not included)

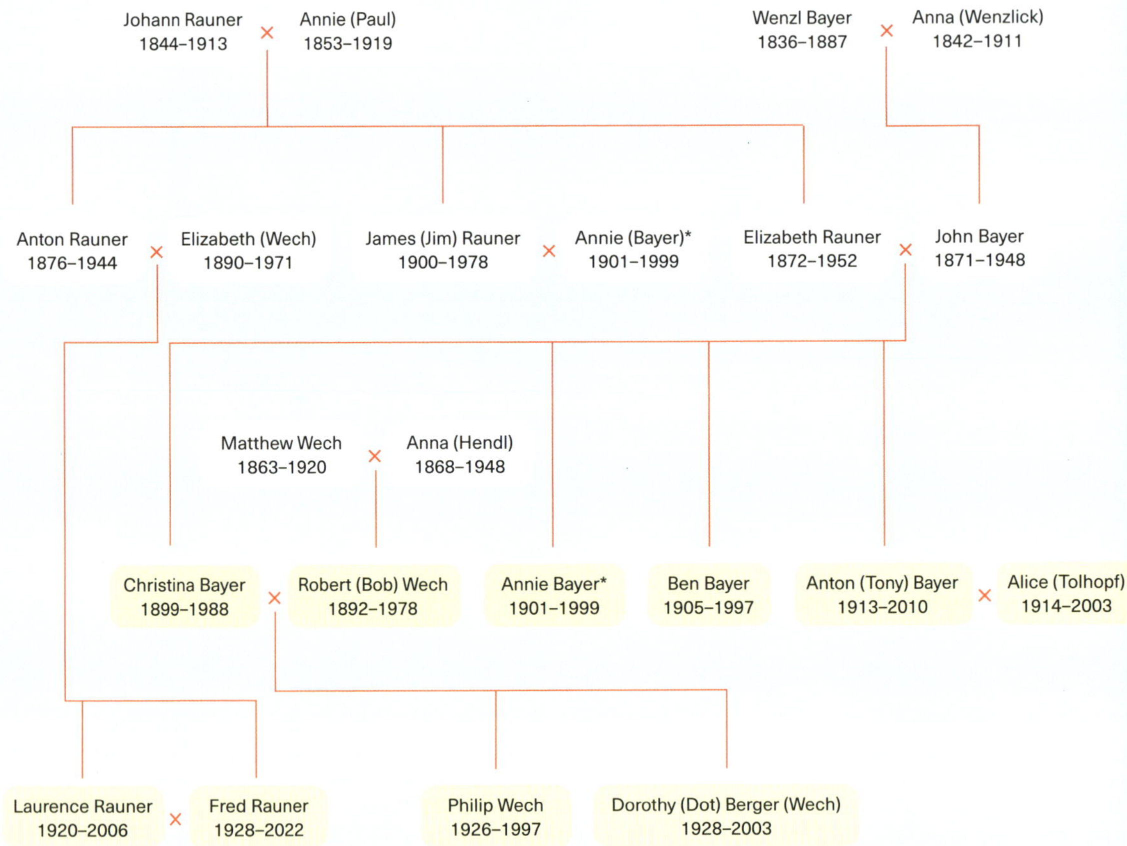

Shaded boxes indicate informants for this study

It is people who make music, and it follows that singing as a shared activity would be attached to social events, such as attending church. This is true for all communities. In the very early European settlement of New Zealand, a repertoire of sea shanties and gold-mining songs developed, sung by men isolated from society. These were to become part of New Zealand's 19th-century folksong heritage. Māori quickly learned the European style of singing, creating new waiata, some of which in turn became popular songs sung by Pākehā; for example, *Pōkarekare Ana.*

For later European settlers, it was the family that provided the most obvious form of social cohesion and there are many accounts of home music-making by the Bohemians, both in their homeland and at Pūhoi. Musical interest and talent continued in those families that had the interest and enthusiasm to enjoy and cultivate it.

In 1996, Fred Rauner described dancing at home:

> They danced in the kitchen when they had a party. They took the big table out and stood it on the grass. It was quite a problem, because it was a big table because we all sat round it, eight of us . . . And they took everything out of the kitchen and then they rolled the mats up and danced.
>
> And the floor used to go up and down, you know, the house blocks were rotten, because the part of the house we were in . . . was only an A-frame made of kauri, [there were] no rooms in it when my mother and father got married . . . Then when Dad and Mum got married in 1912 they only divided it into rooms and put a lean-to for the kitchen and that kitchen part is where they danced back then.[24]

It was the dialect song repertoire that provided the music for dance. Whether it was played or sung is unknown, probably a bit of both. In Pūhoi, there is a commemorative plaque recognising the contribution to Pūhoi music of the families Bayer, Becher, Binsted, Jackson, Krippner, Lambert, Paul, Rauner, Tolhopf, Wech and Yesensky. These families are also celebrated in Maureen Roase's informative and genial book, *Making Melody: Puhoi 1863–2001.* Many of the song and rhyme informants for this collection came from the ranks of these families.

The Straka-Titford families

Not all the families of Pūhoi played music and sang as a way of life. But there were those who conversed in the dialect, remembered and shared the old sayings, and perhaps sang only occasionally. These people also valued Deitsch as a vital part of their culture and heritage.

The Straka and Remiger families had come to New Zealand in 1863. At that time, Paul Straka (1830–1895) was 33 years of age and his future wife, Maria Podlesak (Mary Botelsak) (1840–1927) was 23. Their land allotments adjoined and so they were neighbours. It must have worked well because by 1864 they were married, just one year after arrival. Paul and Maria had seven children including Charles (1870–1948), who was born in 1870. Charles's childhood would have been almost entirely in a dialect-speaking household.

Charles Straka married Theresia Remiger (1879–1972) in 1898; her family had also arrived in 1863. Their children included Ben Straka (1907–1996), who would have also been brought up using Deitsch. Nevertheless, by the time of Ben's birth, the school was going well and the curriculum was taught completely in English. Perhaps family life was also becoming more bilingual, but Ben, a third-generation immigrant, was still fluent in the dialect.

For these families, the dialect survived and thrived when both parents spoke it as a native language. But the situation was different for Isabel Titford (1919–2007), who was destined to marry young Ben Straka.

Isabel's great-grandfather was the Englishman James Titford (1828–1869) who had immigrated to New Zealand sometime before 1863. It is not known exactly when he met Maria Schischka (née Lambert, then Titford, 1838–1908), who had arrived in 1863. Maria was deaf and we do not know when they met and indeed how they communicated when they did, as Maria almost certainly spoke no English.

They must have met soon after Maria's arrival because by 1865 they had married and had a son, James (1865–1958). He was just three years of age when his father drowned in a boating accident on the Waiwera River. So it seems that for two years young James would have been brought up by his deaf Bohemian mother before she married another Englishman, William Lambert, in 1871. They had two children, Wenzl and Mary, step-siblings to James. We cannot be certain which language was spoken at home, but Maria's taste for Englishmen suggests she understood some English even though it is reported that she did not speak the language.

Above: Music in the parlour in Bohemia, 1890s. This image is from a postcard and possibly shows the same instrumentalists as on p. 20. *Michael Cwach*

Below: Honositz, the village of the Straka family, in 2023. This wooden-framed and roofed baroque chapel has a medieval floorplan. Behind the chapel is a row of early 20th-century houses in the Bohemian style. *Michael Cwach*

An expression of faith

All the people who emigrated from Bohemia to settle Pūhoi were Roman Catholic and their faith was integral to their everyday lives. In almost every Bohemian village there was a church and Christian shrines are still numerous on roadsides and in tiny villages there. There is one as you enter Pūhoi.

The settlers arrived in Auckland on Saturday 27 June 1863 and the next day they went to Mass at St Patrick's Cathedral (today known as the Cathedral of St Patrick and St Joseph) in central Auckland to ask Bishop Pompallier to send a priest to their new community. On arriving in Pūhoi, a room in one of the nīkau whare erected by the government for their shelter was set aside as a chapel. In this chapel, the new migrants said the Rosary together and prayed in their family groups.

It was 18 months before Father d'Acherman, who could understand their language, called on his way around the Northern Division, a parish extending from Auckland's North Shore to Whangārei. Other priests paid biannual visits to Pūhoi until Bishop Steins came and was met with an urgent appeal for a resident priest. As a result, in 1877, Pūhoi was named as the centre of the northern parish and Father Adelaar, who also understood their language, became Pūhoi's first resident priest.

Money was immediately collected to build him a presbytery and it is in keeping with the staunch Catholic background of the Bohemian people that this was their first consideration. Efforts to find a priest to visit them and to provide a living space for him were automatic, as important as finding a water supply.

But with such a large parish to cover, Father Adelaar was not in residence very often and Mass was held in the school building twice a month. In 1880, he urged the people to build a church.

John Wenzlick took up the leadership for this task and a marathon community effort began. Subscriptions were collected from Pūhoi, Warkworth and Auckland amounting to £250/18/6. Architect Mr Wrigley designed the building and the people gave timber, their labour and time, and those that had them, the use of their bullocks, horses and drays. Women and children were also involved in this community construction and a child's footprints can be seen in the varnish of the

Above: Church of Saints Peter and Paul, Pūhoi, c. 1890s. *PHS 2657*

Below: A double wedding at Pūhoi joining the Pankratz–Kaes and Titford–Schollum families, c. 1890s. *PHS 1580*

The Pūhoi valley in 2013 with the Church of Saints Peter and Paul in the foreground. Opened in 1881, the church was named after the church in Littitz, Bohemia, which John Wenzlick had attended. *Roger Buckton*

roof sarking. It was truly a labour of love; their Lord transforming their untrained efforts into a magnificent building which still stands as a monument to their faith.

The church was blessed and opened on 10 August 1881. It was named the Church of Saints Peter and Paul after the church in Littitz, Bohemia, that John Wenzlick had attended and because the day the settlers arrived in Pūhoi, 29 June, was the Feast of Saints Peter and Paul. This day has been celebrated in Pūhoi every year since.

Was the Pūhoi dialect spoken formally at church? There are no remaining written records, but we can assume that the Mass at least would have been celebrated in Latin, in keeping with the practice of the Catholic Church at that time (the switch to English occurred in the 1970s).

Jenny Schollum

Ben and Isobel Straka, c. 1980s. *PHS 4783*

James Titford junior (1865–1968) married Mary Schollum (1863–1954) in 1891 (Mary had been born to Bohemian parents). Mary's childhood language must have been in the dialect but by 1891 she would have surely had a working knowledge of English since her father had opened a business in Auckland as general-produce sales merchants, John Schollum and Sons. James and Mary's third child Fred (1893–1968) married Margaret Wenzlick (1896–1982) in 1918. Margaret's grandparents had come from Bohemia and arrived some time between 1866 and 1875, so it is likely that they still conversed in the dialect.

Isabel (1919–2007) was the oldest of nine children of Fred and Margaret Titford. Isabel married Ben Straka in 1948 and Gerard was their first son. Gerard and his sister, Mary, described their mother's command of the dialect as good and certainly functional, but that she never developed the fluency of their father Ben. She could understand it better than she could speak it, but given the presence of English in the Titford family tree, this is hardly surprising! Together, Ben and Gerard actively worked to keep the dialect alive, notably through the website http://www.puhoidialect.net.nz, which provides significant lists of vocabulary and sayings in the dialect spoken by Ben.[25]

The family tree on p. 142 illustrates the familial connection between the Straka–Titford family and the Rauner–Bayer family (p. 132). Maria Podlesak's younger sister, Margaret(ha) (1843–1923), married Joseph Hendl (1848–1934) in Bohemia in 1874. With their two daughters, Anna and Maria, they immigrated to New Zealand on the ship *Friedeburg*, which departed Hamburg on 10 May and arrived in Napier on 24 August 1875. Anna Hendl (1868–1948) married Matthew Wech (1863–1988) and their children included Robert (Bob) Wech (1892–1978), who is also shown in the Rauner–Bayer family tree. This is a wonderful illustration of how all these New Zealand Bohemians are interrelated somehow.

Joseph Paul was born at Poppowa 9 (see also p. 129) on 6 March 1825. He had come to New Zealand in 1863 on the *War Spirit* with his wife and two girls, Anna aged 10 and Katherina aged 3. Annie (also Anna) later married Johann Rauner (see p. 129) and they had 17 children. John and Wenzl Paul came to New Zealand on the *Shakespeare*, arriving in Wellington (from Hamburg) on 23 January 1876. Aged 17 and 19 respectively, they were with seven other siblings as part of the family of Michael and Maria Paul from Blatnice, near Pilsen. Michael was the younger brother of Joseph Paul.

Charles Becher (1874–1956), a builder by trade, was a significant Pūhoi musician who could read music and wrote many of the old Bohemian tunes in his manuscript book, which has been an important source for this collection.

Left: Joseph Paul (c. 1890). *PHS 0829*

Below: A triple wedding in Pūhoi on 16 April 1901. The musicians (left to right): Joseph Paul (dudelsack), John Paul (violin) and Wenzl Paul (accordion). The bridegrooms and brides (left to right): Charles Becher and Catherine Schollum, Joseph Schollum and Mary Lambert, John Karl and Elizabeth Remiger. *PHS 0983*

Informants from the Straka–Tilford families showing links to the Wech family

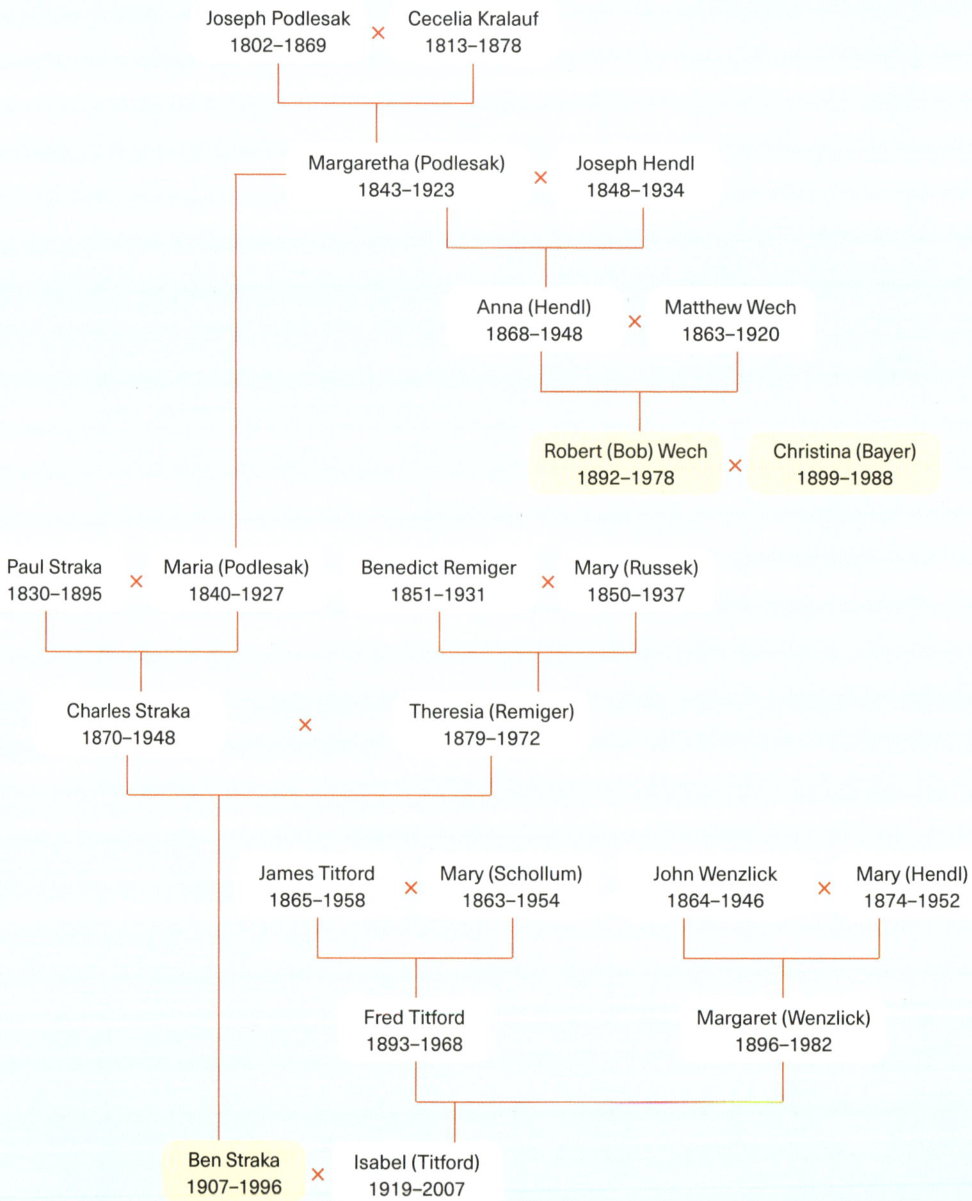

Shaded boxes indicate informants for this study

Anna Becher (née Podlesak), seated, with three of her children, Cecelia (Lilian) and Joe (standing), and Charles Becher. *PHS 1160*

The Podlesak sisters

Joseph Podlesak (1802–1869) and Cecelia (Kralauf) (1813–1878) lived in Bohemia and had nine children. Their only son did not survive infancy and of their eight daughters, four immigrated to New Zealand in an example of what is known as chain migration, where family members are encouraged to migrate by those who have already made the move. Anna (1833–1913), aged 25, came with her husband, Thomas Becher (1983–1890), and their two children on the *War Spirit* in 1863. Two younger sisters, Maria, aged 23, and Elizabeth, aged 15, joined them. Later, in 1876, Anna's sister Margaretha (1843–1923), with her husband Joseph Hendl (1848–1834) and their two children, arrived in New Zealand on the ship *Friedeberg*.

Anna and Thomas Becher were the parents of Charlie Becher (seated above), whose music manuscript book is a source of many of the melodies reproduced here, and Margaret (Margaretha) and Joseph's daughter Anna was the mother of Robert (Bob) Wech, who was another source for a number of the songs.

APPENDIX

Song origins and text variations

When a song was being sung in Pūhoi in the Deitsch in the 1960s, the likelihood is that it is a song from the old country of Egerland and has been remembered over the generations. If so, it is probable that the same song can be still found in Europe. So, a European source can be found for every song in this collection except for one, *Meck, meck, d' Zeng is gfreckt*. The fact that this song cannot be found in European sources could mean that it has simply become lost over time or that in fact it was composed in New Zealand.

For all the other songs, with the passage of time and variations in dialect and language invariably no song in a European source will be exactly the same as the Pūhoi version. The following section provides additional background for each song, its sources in Europe, together with some alternative versions. Sometimes more verses have been provided and, with adaption, these could be useful for performance. Extra verses usually give more meaning to the song as a whole. Sometimes the 'punchline' is in the final verse, as in *Håns gäih huom* (p. 84).

Where text variations are given, they are in the dialect unless otherwise indicated.

Nao an Winta kinnt da Summa *page 28*

This song, which developed in Germany at the end of the 19th century, is an example of a Gstanzl (see p. 29). Georg Queri (1912, p. 109) mentions another Gstanzl in the context of when a boy visits a girl:

Middle Bavarian dialect	*English*
Steht a Wetter am Himmi	If there is a thunderstorm in the sky
aber donnern tuats net,	but it doesn't thunder,
steig i eini beim Fenster,	I'll step in through the window,
aber lärma derfst net.	but don't make a noise.

One of the singers and warrantors for this song was Pius Honis, born in Neuern (Czech: Nýrsko) in the Bohemian Forest not far from the Bavarian border and southwest of Pilsen. After World War II, he brought many tunes and songs from his home to the region north of Regensburg, in the district of Upper Palatinate.

O du schäina Summablouma *page 30*

This type of song is a priamel, a joke poem with four verses from the late medieval period. *O du schäina Summablouma* is a variation of *O du schöne Sonnenblume*, which was known in south and middle Germany in the neighbourhood of the Egerland.

High German	*English*
Ei du schöne Sonnenblume,	O you pretty sunflower,
du hast mir mein Herz genomme,	you've taken my heart,
du liegst mir in meinem Sinn	you are in my mind
wie der Kern im Kümmerling.	like the seed in the *Kümmerling.* (a black cucumber)

The song was also collected by Ludwig Erk (1894, p. 415) in Eschborn near Wiesbaden. It is also known in the Erzgebirge (a region next to the Egerland in the north) and in Thüringen.

In Czech, the song was collected by J. Jindřich (1926–1930) in Chodsko.

Czech	*English*
Má panenko, jak se máš,	My darling, how are you,
sili zdráva, co děláš,	are you well, what are you doing,
Sili zdráva, co pa' děláš?	are you well, what are you doing now?
Pověz ty mně,	Tell me,
ja'pa' se máš,	how are you,
sili zdráva?	are you well?
Co děláš, pověz ty mně,	What are you doing, tell me?
jak se máš?	how are you?

It is different in textual meanings to the German versions, but it is the same tune.

Baua heng dai(n) Bumml ua(n) *page 34*

Text variations of this song are in 'Bauer bind dein Pudel an' in *Deutsches Kinderlied und Kinderspiel* (1897) while the rural areas of Mühlviertel in Austria (Derschmidt, 1985) and Transdanubia in Hungary (Kiss, 1979) provide further regional variations.

Transdubian	
1, 2, 3, 4, 5, 6, 7,	1, 2, 3, 4, 5, 6, 7,
helft mir doch den Schiebbock schieben.	help mc push this barrow
Wo denn hin?	Where to?
Auf Berlin [oder Stadt Wien etc.]	To Berlin [or Vienna etc.]
setz dich drauf und fahr mit hin.	Get on and come with me.

Bauer häng dein Pudel an,	Farmer tie up your poodle,
daß er mich nicht beißen kann.	so he can't bite me.
Beißt er mich, verklag ich dich,	If he bites me, I'll sue you,
Tausend Taler kost' es dich.	Thousand Taler, it will cost you.

There is another variation from the Volga Republic (1763–1941) in Russia, a region which once had 104 German-speaking villages and towns.[18]

German	*English*
Bauer, bind dem Pudel an,	Farmer tie your poodle (a large black dog)
Dass er mich nicht beißen kann.	So that he can't bite me.
Beißt er mich, verklag ich dich,	If he bites me, I'll sue you,
Hundert Rubel kostet's dich.	Hundred Rubel it will cost you.

Giekerl, wennst du niat krahst *page 36*

Just the melody of this song remained in Pūhoi, but it is similar to the Czech song *Já si tě, nevez mu*. The tune is also similar to a German folksong in Bavaria. As the early immigrants of Pūhoi came from a region between both the Czech and Bavarian populations, they would have had contact with their neighbours, but we cannot be certain from whom the tune was adapted. If from the Bavarian side, the text was not used in Pūhoi and the tune has varied over time, so that the former text no longer fits. For this version, the text from North Bavaria neighbouring the Egerland was used.

Bist denn du bäis? *page 40*

Bergmann (1952) and Sykora (1976) provide the whole narrative. The context is that the boy knocks at the girl's window, but she doesn't open it to let him in.

Bergmann / Sykora	
Moidal, bist bäis, owa moghst mi niat?	Girl, are you angry or don't you love me?
Owa san dös deina Fenza niat?	Or are these not your windows?
Owa san dös deina Fenza niat?	Or are these not your windows?
Ich bin niat bäis, ich häias scho.	I am not angry, I can hear you.
Du håust an Rausch, dös woiß i scho.	You are tipsy, that I know.
Du håust an Rausch, dös woiß i scho.	You are tipsy, that I know.
Ho(w) i an Rausch, dös mecht da Wei(n).	If I am tipsy, it is from the wine.

Schåtzerl, stäih af u lau mi ei(n).	Get up, my dear, and let me come in.
Schåtzerl, stäih af u lau mi ei(n).	Get up, my dear, and let me come in.
Ich stäih niat af, låu di niat ei(n)	I won't get up, won't let you come in,
Du könnst hei(n)t Nåcht ma Unglück sa.	You could be my ruin this night.
Du könnst hei(n)t Nåcht ma Unglück sa.	You could be my ruin this night.
Moidal, gäih schau, i ho di gern.	Girl, look here, I like you a lot.
Du moußt gånz gwiß ma Wei(b) nu wer(d)n.	You shall surely be my wife one day.
Du moußt gånz gwiß ma Wei(b) nu wer(d)n.	You shall surely be my wife one day.
D' Boum, döi san fålsch, u sua vadraht.	The boys are wily and so twisted.
Grod wöi as Laba da Wind herwaht.	Like the wind that blows the leaves around.
Grod wöi as Laba da Wind herwaht.	Like the wind that blows the leaves around.

An alternative version is in Hofmann (1901) as follows:

Wenn i hei(n)t Nåcht da Unglück bin,	If I should be your ruin this night,
gäng ma mitanånna zan Pfårra hin,	then let's go together to the priest,
gäng ma mitanånna zan Pfårra hin.	then let's go together to the priest.
Gäng ma zan Pfårra zan Kåppaloan,	Let's go to the priest, to the chaplain,
I kröigh a Wei(b) und du an Moa(n).	I'll get a wife and you a husband.
I kröigh a Wei(b) und du an Moa(n).	I'll get a wife and you a husband.

The recording from Pūhoi (1963) is not the same as Bergmann (1952) and Sykora (1976). A similar tune to the Pūhoi version is in a song (1913) from Neumarkt (Czech: Úterý) not far from the Pūhoi settlers' home area. The title of this song is *Lernt a Kind nix*, but there is a completely different text. It is reproduced in *Liederbuch der Egerländer* (Bergmann, 1952). Bergmann took the song from *Egerländer Volkslieder 2* (Czerny and Alois, 1901).

The same version can be found in *Singendes Egerland. Ein- und zweistimmige Egerländer Lieder* (Sykora and Reiter, 1976). Bergmann also quotes Josef Hofmann in *Deutsche Volkslieder aus Böhmen*, Josef Sykora and Mochl Reiter, 1976.

Za di bin i gånga *page 42*

This song is from Egerland, Böhmerwald (a low mountain range on the German–Czech border), Austria and Bavaria with different texts and more than one melody line. In Brosch (1997) the song has the same text but different melodies from its reproduction in Eger

(1940), Tachau (1910–1928), and Plan (1894) in Urban (1894), and Franzenbad (1901) in Czerny and Alois (1901). The Pūhoi tune most resembles the tune from Eger.

In west Bohemia, there was a small town, Plan (Czech: Planá), quite close to the Pūhoi settlers' origins in Chotieschau and Mies. From there comes this variation (Hruschka and Toischer, 1891). It is shown in the dialect of the area.

Za dia bin i ganga, ba dia haut's mi gfreit. Za dia gäih ich nimma, der Wegh is ma z'weit.	To you did I venture, with you I had joy. But now I don't come anymore, the way is too far.
Da Wegh is ma z'weit u da Wald is ma z'dick. B'hoit di Gott ma(n) lois Schatzerl, Ich wünsch da vül Glück.	The way is too far and the forest too thick. God bless you, my dear darling, I wish you good luck.
Ich wünsch da vül Glück, u's soll da gout gäi(h)n. Füa(r) Zeit, wo'st mi g'löibt haust, bedank ich mi schäi(n).	I wish you good luck, and may it go well with you. I thank you so much, for the time you have loved me.
Ich bedank mi recht schäi(n), füa d'Löi u füa d'Trei. Füa d'Falschheit owa a, döi woa(r) oft dabei.	I thank you kindly, for your love and loyalty. But also for the falseness too, that was often there.

From Bavaria, Queri (1912) wrote that this song describes the age-old practice of boys secretly visiting girls at night.

Zu dir bin ih ganga drei ganzi Wocha, bal ih nomal zu dir geh, wer ih heilih gspocha.	To you did I venture three whole weeks, if I visit you again, I'll be canonised.
Aba zu dir bin ich ganga bein Regn und bein Wind und zu dir geh ich nimma, weil an andana kimmt!	But I ventured to you in all kinds of weather and now I won't come again, because another [boy] visits you!

For an Austrian version see Webinger (1929).

Duarl haot g'sågt (Straka version) *page 44–47*

This is a song of youth and age, summer and winter. In the first verse, Dora says the plums are good. Known since at least the time of the Renaissance as a metaphor for fertility, this is indicating the time is ripe for children. But in the second verse, 'my winter' has arrived and Dora is now too old to have children. This song was well known in the Egerland and is also noted in Köferl (1895), Brosch (1997), Urban (1894), and Hruschka and Toischer (1891).

Der wos döi bayrisch Duarl will hom *page 48*

This song was collected from the Gubernial collection in Prague by Thomas Kunz (1825) (recorded in Tyllner, 1995). Another publication of the same song was made by Johann von Rittersberg in 1825 (compare with Baumann 1984 and Baumann, 1985).

The song can be seen in later collections: Czerny and John (1901), Bergmann (1952), Brosch (1997), Heil (1963), and Sykora and Reiter (1976). Braun (2004) has the whole, almost identical text: *Ei wer die båirisch Duarl wüll hoo(b)m, der mou a såmmats Kappl aaf hoo(b)m! A såmmats Kappl, a sülwas Påar Schnååln, dees wird da båirisch'n Duarl scho gfååľn*!

The song with the same tune and another text is located in the Bavarian neighbourhood of Oberpfalz (Upper Palatinate) as *Wer mir und meiner Schwårzn wås tout*, compare Eichenseer and Mayer (1976). The Egerlander version is printed there as a text variation together with another verse. *Bayrisch* means Bavarian but also *bäuerisch* (farmer). Probably, all text versions had Bavarian in mind, but it also makes sense to think of a farmer's daughter.

If a man wants to marry a farmer's daughter, he should be a farmer himself, not a farm worker or farmhand or a craftsman or an inhabitant of a city. This social status aspect is supported by the farmer's costume which includes a velvet cap and silver shoe buckles. Many old pictures show Egerlanders with velvet caps worn inside the house while outside the men typically wore hats (Heimrath, 2002).

Dra Åckarla Kraat *page 50*

Erich Baumann collected this song from Laurie Rauner in 1984 and published it in *Egerländer Volkslieder* in 1990. It had previously been included in Urban (1894) and Hruschka/Wendelin (1891).

Meck, meck, d' Zeng is gfreckt and Däi Schul håst du ålla aaf dia *page 52*

To date, no European sources or references have been found for these songs.

Ha(n)sl Bou *page 56*

Hasl is the original *Hansl* (Johnny). *Bub* is the southern German word for northern German *Junge* (boy). Baumann (1990) notes that it is an old Egerlander song from the 19th century and provides a second verse. The song is also in Brosch (1997) and he notes that it was collected in Eger in 1935.

Wiewadl, wawadl, was is das? *page 62*

Bieberl or *Wiewerl/Wiewadl* means young goose (Braun, 2004; Denz, 1977) or chicken (Zehetner, 1998). The Pūhoi songs recorded by Werner Droescher have a mistake in the rhyme lines 1 and 3. In Braun (2004) the correct song in a south Egerlander dialect is as follows:

Wiewadl, Waawadl, was ist das,	Wiewadl wawadl what is that?
Hinta da Höll* dao kråbblt was;	Behind the hell something is crawling;
's is kua(n) Fuks, und 's is kua(n) Haas,	It's not a fox and not a bunny.
Wiewadl, waawadl, was ist das?	Wiewadl wawadl what is that?

* *Höll* (hell) is the hottest place in a farmer's house; it is in the corner next to the tile stove where the newborn chickens were kept in a cage.

Unna Vetta Veitl *page 64*

This is a common children's song with some text variations, compare Brosch (1997). There are many verses in Brosch, employing several boys' names, but not in the Pūhoi version. Brosch no. 1734 is also in Hruschka and Toischer (1891) and is an old variation collected in Plan (Czech: Planá) not far from the Pūhoi settlers' home area. Brosch no. 1733 also appears in Bergmann (1952) and in Sykora and Reiter (1976).

Braun (2004) has the text in the North Egerland dialect with a version similar to the Pūhoi version. Jungbauer (1899) has a text variation used in the Böhmerwald, a German-speaking region south of the Egerland (Pimmer, 1976).

In d'Stod eifoahrn *page 70*

The text is taken from Eichenseer and Karrer (1999). The song has the same melody as the Pūhoi tune in the medley *Summer Air in May* and was recorded by Adolf J. Eichenseer in 1990 and 1998. One of the singers was Pius Honis from Neuern (Czech: Nýrsko), southwest of the region where the Pūhoi settlers came from. He brought the song from his home in Bohemia to Bavaria. The other two singers are from Upper Palatinate, Bavaria.

Schwaza Pfaala raid ge(r)an *page 72*

This song is a *Gstanzl*, a popular type of humorous song and mostly with four lines and enjoyed in the pub. These songs can make much use of the double entendre and any text which implies various parts of a female body in a frivolous sense is fair game. Verse 1 is also in Braun (2004).

In Northern Germany, a variation of this text is known in a song for children:

Rote Kirschen ess ich gern,
schwarze noch viel lieber.
In die Schule geh ich gern,
alle Tage wieder.

I like to eat red cherries,
but much more black cherries.
I love to go to school
every day again.

O du löiwa Augustin *page 74*

The text and meaning of this song go back to about 1670, when a poor drunk bagpiper in Vienna fell into the gutter after visiting a pub. By 1800 the song had spread over the whole of Europe (Nagel, 2016). Rudolf Flotzinger writes in the *Oesterreichisches Musiklexikon online* (Austrian music encyclopedia online) that the song is first documented about 1800 as a theatre song in Bohemia: *Honza Kolohnát z Přelouče* [Hanns Klachel from Przelautsch] by Vinzenz F. Tuczek according to Karl Franz Guolfinger v. Steinsberg, 1795/97 Prag, Teplitz. It's a memorable and catchy tune so there are many text variations ranging from the gutter song to the Kiwi kids' song *The more we are together the happier we will be.*

In Brosch (1997) there is a text variation entitled *Da Augustin* noted as collected from Eger in 1937 with the following text:

O du löiwa Augustin, d' Kåtz is in da Röiha drin,
håut si(ch) die gãnza Haut vabrennt, schaut 's nea wöi sie rennt,

O my dear Augustin, the cat is in the oven,
has burnt itself the whole skin, look how it runs.

Wei, tou an Säusook her, Ich ho nan in da Röiha gseah.	Wife, give me a pork roast, I saw it in the oven.
Wei, tou an Säusook her, Ich ho nan schoň gseah.	Wife, give me a pork roast, I've already seen it.
Bist du niat a ålwara Moaň,	Aren't you a foolish man
siahst d' Kåtz für n Säusook oaň!	you see the cat as pork roast!
Is dös niat a ålwara Moaň, schaut 's nan nea(r) oaň.	Isn't he a foolish man, just look at him.

The song was also known to the German settlers in the former Volga Republic in Russia (Spack, 2010). In England the song is known as *O my dear friend Augustin*, and in the USA there is a children's song *Ach, du lieber Augustin . . . all is kaputt / money gone, honey gone / my goose is cooked* (Nagel, 2016).

Wenn häit ma(n) Mutta ma(n) Huasn niat g'flickt *page 76*

Two recordings made by Gerard Straka in Pūhoi in 2009 with the singers Ben Straka and Fred Rauner have almost the same text:

Wenn häit ma(n) Mutta ma(n) Huisn niat g'flickt	Wenn häit ma(n) Mutta ma(n) Huisn niat g'flickt,
sou waar e gonga -r-in Hem,	åffa waar e gonga -r-in Hem,
sou waar e gonga -r-in Hem,	åffa waar e gonga -r-in Hem,
Wenn häit mi ma(n) Mutta ma(n) Huisn niat g'flickt	Wenn häit mi ma(n) Mutta ma(n) Huisn niat g'flickt,
sou waar e gonga -r-in Hem, Hem, Hem	åffa waar e gonga -r-in Hem, Hem, Hem
(Straka)	(Rauner)

There are textual variations: *häit mi, Huisn, sou waar e gonga. Huisn* is rarely used, *Huasn* is more common.

The song is the second verse of a song formerly sung in Southern Egerland entitled *Siada, dass i gheirat hoh(b)* (Since I have married). The first of six verses is:

Siada, dass i gheirat hoo(b,	Since I have married
dees is a kurza Zeit,	a short time before,
dees is a kurza Zeit,	a short time before,
dees is a kurza Zeit.	a short time before.
Mei(n Huasn san ma schlåmpat woa(rd)n,	My trousers got sloppy,
ma Leiwl is ma z' weit,	my jerkin is too wide,

ma Leiwl is ma z' weit,	my jerkin is too wide,
holdrio	holdrio.

The whole song is printed in Baumann (1990). The second verse from Pūhoi is slightly different from the Egerland version. In Northern Bavaria, next to the Czech border, there is a song *Uner alte Waawer* (Kreger, 2002) respectively *Unser ålte Wawa* (Eichenseer, 2014, and Eichenseer and Karrer, 2009). It has the same melody as *Wenn häit ma(n) Mutta ma(n) Huasn niat g'flickt.*

Waawer is an Egerlander dialectal loanword from Czech *baba* which means grandmother or old woman (similar to Russian *babuschka*). The song is a typical *Gstanzl* (also known as a *Schnadahüpfl*). This type is very common as a pub song. It has often four lines and a 3/4 or 2/4 bar. There are a lot of tunes for *Gstanzl* in different dialects. In a performance, one singer sings a verse and another singer invents a new verse in reply. The content of a *Gstanzl* is ironic and is good for a laugh. Good *Gstanzl* are repeated and so they spread (Eichenseer, 2014).

I u ma(n ålts Wei *page 82*

An old version, recorded in 1913, from the 19th century is printed in Baumann (1990). Similar to the Pūhoi version, this provides a basis for the song without the addition of the extra line from *Heißa Kathreinerle* as shown on the song page.

I u ma(n ålts Wei(b, kina schäi(n tånz(n.	Me and my old wife can dance well.
Si mit(n) Bee(d)lsook, i mi(t)n Rånz(n.	She with the beggar's bag, I with the knapsack.
Si gäiht åll Toogh in d Stood, Dåu mou(ß si laff(n,	She goes every day to the city and she has to on foot,
Woos si dabee(d)lt håut, tou I vasaff(n.	What she has begged, I waste it on drink.
I u ma(n ålts Wei(b, mia(r leb(m niat üwl.	Me and my old wife, we don't live bad.
Wenn ma koa(n Schmoolz niat hoo(b)m, ess ma asn Küwl.	When we don't have shortening, we eat from the bucket.

Text variations:

1. The text in Baumann (1990) is the same as Brosch (1997); the tune is also the same except for the last bar.

2. Brosch (1997) is a variation in text and tune and Brosch (1997) is a text variation. The tune seems to be a second part to no. 1409. There are versions in Brosch (1997), Band 3. All have music.

3. The song was also collected from Iglau (Czech: Jihlava), which was a German-language island in a Czech-speaking area about 250 kilometres east of Mies (Czech: Stříbro).

Iglau	*English*
I und mei junges Weib	Me and my young wife
Können gut tanza.	We can dance well.
Sie mit'n Bettelsack,	She with the beggar's bag,
I mit'n Ranza.	I with the knapsack.
I und mei altes Weib,	Me and my old wife,
Wir leben nit übel;	we don't live too badly;
Sie verkauft d' Schuh und d' Strümpf,	She sells shoes and socks,
I meine Stiefel.	I my boots.
Sie geht in d' Stadt hinein,	She goes into the town,
I bleib halt draußen;	But I'm staying outside;
Was sie derbetteln thut,	The money she gets from begging,
Thu I versaufen.	I waste on drink.

This song in the form A-B-A has the same A section as the folksong *Heißa Kathreinerle*. The tune has its roots in the German-speaking parts of Alsace in the 14th century. The text from about 1928 is a replacement for *Gügük im Häfele*, published by Weckerlin in 1883. The middle section (Didel dudel dadel shrum shrum shrum) was added in the late 19th century (cf. Ziemann (2013): *Heißa Kathreinerle, schnür' dir die Schuh*).

I u man ålts Wie may be found in a number of sources from German-speaking areas of Europe. In Ukraine, the largest nuclear power-plant in Europe is at Zaporizhia on the river Dnieper. A short distance away, on the other side of the river, is the Ukrainian city of Nikopol, where there once lived a German-speaking minority who sang this song.

Hans gäih huom *page 84*

Gerard Straka (2009), compare Heimrath (2015), recorded his father, Ben Straka in Pūhoi as follows:

Hans gäih huam,	John go home,
ma wois jå niad, wäi 's Weda wiad wern,	one doesn't know what the weather will be,
sou Hans gäih huam.	so John go home.
Kännt renga kennt schnaia,	Could be raining or snowing,
sou Hans gäih huam.	so John go home.

This pub song about John is well known in southern Germany. John wants to go home to his wife but his drinking friends ask him to stay and call him a hen-pecked husband. The result is that John stays drinking with his friends!

The text for all the verses in this version follows:

Deitsch	*English*
Håns blai dao, du woisd jå niad, wäi 's Weda wiad. Håns blai dao, du woisd jå niad, wäi 's wiad,	John stay here, you don't know what the weather will be. John stay here, you don't know what it will be,
Es kua(n) renga oda schnai(b)m, oda-r a schäi(n)s Weda blai(b)m, Håns blai dao, du woisd jå niad, wäi 's wiad.	Could be raining, could be snowing, could be nice weather, John stay here, you don't know what it will be.
I mou hoam, jå wail ma(n) Waiwerl woad aaf mi, I mou hoam, jå wail ma(n) Waiwerl woad. Sie håd gsågd, wenn i niad kimm, möisd i wieda Schaitl* knien, I mou hoam, jå wail ma(n) Waiwerl woad.	I have to go home, because my wife is waiting for me, I have to go home, because my wife is waiting. She said, if I wouldn't come, I would have to kneel on kindling wood* again, I have to go home, because my wife is waiting.
Gäih nua zou, du bisd jå a Bandoflhöld, gäih nua zou, du Bandoflhöld. Gäih no zu dain Waiwerl hoam, mia, mia måchn duach bis morng, Gäih nua zou, du Bandoflhöld, gäih nua zou.	Yes, go home, you are a hen-pecked husband, go home, hen-pecked husband. Just go to your wife, we ourselves will continue till tomorrow morning. Just go, hen-pecked husband, just go.
I blai(b) dou, i hamma 's anders übalegt. I blai(b) dou, i hamma 's übalegt. 'S Wai kua(n) schimpfa oda schraia, i blai(b) löiwa dao und faia. i blai(b) dou, i hamma 's übalegt.	I'll stay here, I've changed my mind. I'll stay here, I have reconsidered. The wife can scold or cry, I would rather stay and have a party. I'll stay here, I've changed my mind.

*Schaitl (Holzscheite) or kindling wood. Kneeling on kindling was a common punishment in earlier days.

A south Egerland version is in Baumann (1990) with sources from Gustav Jungbauer (1913), Hruschka and Toischer (1891). Another variation without text is in Baumann (1985) entitled *Seff bei(b dåu.* The *Tirschenreuther Liedermappe* vol. 4 (Kreger, 2002) in Upper Palatinate neighbouring south Egerland has the same variation as Baumann (1990). Yet another version is well performed in the 19th-century style with dudelsack, violin and clarinet on the CD *Gestan bin i assegfoahrn.*

A Räuscherl im Kopf *page 86*

The song is sung in South Germany and Austria and is well known as *Der Vogelbeerbaum* (the rowan tree) and printed in Bergmann (1952); *Bundesliederbuch* (c. 1900); Schötz and Wax (2006); Sykora and Reiter (1976). The popular current text was written by Max Schreyer, probably in 1887 in the region of Erzgebirge (neighbour of Egerland) and first published in 1894 (cf. Blechschmidt, 1981).

Before Max Schreyer's poem, the tune was used in a song published in Vienna (c. 1840) entitled *Zwa harbere Göden* (Two bad godparents), as *A Dampferl im Kopf* (c. 1850) and in 1876, as *Vogtländische Rundä-Melodie,* and also Kremser (1912). The tune is printed as a *Schnadahüpfl* (a type of humorous song) in Kobell (1871), as *Ausseer Walzer* or *Steyrischer Walzer* with the text *Von Wald gehn i außa* (I'm going out of the forest) in Graz, Austria in 1918 (Deutsch, 1979).

Other uses of the tune are again in Graz; *Die lustigen Hammaschmiedsgsölln* (The funny hammer-smith journeymen) in Zach (1887); and Franz Friedrich Kohl (1899).

Eins und zwei und drei und vier *page 88*

This song and dance is well known in Austria, Germany, the German-speaking parts of Western Bohemia and other parts of Europe. It has different names: *Rückwärtspolka* (Backward Polka); *Krebspolka* (Crab Polka); *Manchester Polka; Der Neukatholische* (The new Catholic). Both Egerlanders and people in Pūhoi used the High German version, *Eins, zwei, drei und vier* (One, two, three and four).

The song's origin is in the Alps, where the Middle Bavarian dialect is spoken (including Austrian). This is a good song for making up your own new verses. The names *Rückwärtspolka* and *Krebspolka* indicate that the dancers make backward steps.

The following text is from Upper Palatinate, a neighbouring region to Egerland in Bavaria and in a Middle Bavarian dialect (cf. Eichenseer and Karrer, 1999).

Oans, zwoa, drei und vier,	One, two, three and four,
Dirndl, heb dein Rock auf d'Höh und zoag ma deine Knia.	Girl, lift your skirt and show me your knees.
Fünf, sechs, sieben und acht,	Five, six, seven and eight,
Dirndl, wennst zum Tanzen gehst,	if you are going to the dance,
dann nimm dich fei in Acht.	girl be careful.
Net a so, net a so, wia's die Buama macha,	Not like this, not like this, like the boys do it,
net a so, net a so, des is ja zum Lacha.	not like this, not like this, this makes us laugh.

In Austria, there are two different text traditions in the Middle Bavarian dialect and without a refrain.

Oins, zwoi, drei, väir, fünf, sechs, sieb'n *page 90*

This melody with text variations is still sung in Germany and Austria. It was collected by Adolf König with four verses from North Bohemia (Spurný, 2000).

Verse 1:

Eins, zwei, drei, vier fünf, sechs, sieb'n,	One, two, three, four, five, six, seven,
hilf mir doch den Schiebbock schieb'n.	help me push the barrow.
Wo denn hin? Nach Berlin.	Where to? To Berlin.
Setz dich drauf und fahre hin.	Sit up and go there.

Verse 4 (note the similarity to *Baua heng dai(n) Bumml ua(n)*, p. 34):

Bauer, bind' den Pudel an,	Farmer, tie up your poodle,
daß er mich nicht beißen kann,	so he cannot bite me,
beißt er mich, klag ich dich,	if he bites me, I'll punish you,
Tausend Taler kost't es dich.	It will cost you a thousand Taler.

The similarity in the texts will be observed with *Baua heng dai(n) Bumml ua(n)* (p. 34) and the text of this song can be sung with this *Prince of Wales Schottischer* melody.

An instrumental version of the *Prince of Wales Schottischer* is in Baumann (1985) and is shown on p. 91. The dance is popular as *Siebenschritt* (seven steps) in all German-speaking countries in Europe (Germany, Austria, Switzerland). The tune has been known since the second half of the 18th century and is also used for a common German folksong *Brüderchen, komm tanz mit mir* (Dance with me, my little brother), known since about 1800 and used in Humperdinck's opera *Hänsel und Gretel* from 1893 (Haffner, 1979).

In addition, the tune is in the German children's song *Eins, zwei, drei, vier, fünf, sechs, sieben, wo ist denn mein Schatz geblieben? Ist nicht hier, ist nicht da, ist ja in Amerika.*

Moidl rupf di, zupf di, kämm di schäi(n) *page 92*

Moira is a variation of *Moi(d)la* and means girls in the plural. In the recording, Alice Tolhopf didn't use *Moira,* but the man's question at the beginning has this word. The poem addresses only one girl. Alice had problems singing this text and her sung versions had linguistic issues. In the spoken text, the word *Samdsdou* in line 2 had a partial English pronunciation but the pronunciation was better when they sang it.

It is not clear whether the girl and the person who addresses her are going to be married. The singer says that next Saturday there is a wedding and he/she wants to go there with the addressed girl. In Baumann (1990) there is a text variation:

Måi(d)l rupf di zupf di kämm di schäi(n.	Girl, primp yourself, plait yourself, comb yourself.
Am Sunnta wolln ma am Tånzbuadn gäih(n.	On Sunday, we plan to go to the dance barn.

This version is not complete but it shows that the song has its origins in Egerland. A similar song, *Maadla tu dich putzn,* is recorded in south Germany in the region of Oberfranken (Upper Franconia), neighbouring northern Egerland (Gleichmann, 1933).

Upper Franconian dialect	*English*
Maadla, tu dich putzn,	Girl, primp yourself,
dein Zopf aufschteckn schee,	tie up your hair nicely,
no wolln mer glei zewander	now we will go
fort auf die Musik geh;	together to the dance,
wolln die Schuhsuhln dorchtanzn	we will wear out our shoes by dancing
und lustig, lustig saa,	and be jolly, jolly,
dermit daß uns der Kehraus	so that the last dance
is werklich richtig laa.	is indeed really great.

Finger Polka *page 97*

This polka is one of the popular dances played by the accordion (Williams, 1981). Erich Baumann collected it from Laurie Rauner in 1984 and published it in *Alt-Egerländer Tänze.* Baumann gives other sources — Mies, Staab and Pilsen — suggesting its popularity across this region as well as Bavaria and Lithuania. The German title *Finger Polka* used in Lithuania suggests that the dance either is imported from Germany or was left there by Germans who settled there until the end of World War II. Yet another children's polka version in Wisconsin, United States, is *Annie in the Cabbage Patch* or the Czech *Šla Nanynka do zeli.*

Notes

1 Droescher, W. O. 'The Egerland-German dialect of Puhoi (North Auckland), New Zealand'. 1969. Paper archived in Auckland Public Libraries.

2 The collection is known as the Gubernial Collection and is mainly housed in the State Archives at the Kunsthistorisches Museum, Vienna but also in Prague, Brno and Trebon. The two songs in this collection that are in the Gubernial Collection are *Der wos döi bayrisch Duadl will hom* and *Ha(n)sl Bou*. For more information see: https://image.folkoveprazdniny.cz/2016/kolokvium2016/sbornik2016_04_Toncrova_en.pdf

3 Albert Brosch (1886–1970). For further details see p. 65.

4 The Egerland is an historical and cultural region in the northeast of Bohemia. Today this region is part of the Czech Republic.

5 *New Zealand Herald*, 30 June 1913, p. 9.

6 Salzmann, Zdenek and Vladimír Scheufler, *Komárov: A Czech farming village*. New York: Holt, Rinehart & Winston, 1974.

7 Silk, D. V. *A history of Puhoi*. Dunedin: N.Z. Tablet Printing & Publishing Co., p. 103. Although Silk cites *Auckland News*, 16 December July 1883 as the source of the quote, extensive searching has not been able to locate the origin of this extract.

8 A group of approximately 30 Egerlanders came to Puhoi in 1984, and many visited again in 1988 for the celebration of Pūhoi's 125th anniversary. Smaller groups, including family groups, have come through the years, including about 12 Egerlanders attending the 150th anniversary in 2013. There have also been groups from Pūhoi who have visited Egerland.

9 Gubernial Collection, op.cit.

10 Ibid.

11 Charles Burney (1775), facsimile in Barbara Ann Renton, 'The musical culture of 18th century Bohemia', PhD thesis, City University of New York, 1969.

12 A ländler has a gentle lilting rhythm in 3/4 or triple time. It is a dance for couples and in traditional folk situations is danced in a circle.

13 Droescher, op. cit.

14 Gubernial Collection, op.cit.

15 Salzmann, Zdenek and Vladimír Scheufler, op.cit.

16 *Auckland Weekly News*, 17 February 1872, p. 6.

17 *Daily Southern Cross*, 10 December 1866, p. 5.

18 Droescher, op. cit.

19 Silk, op.cit.

20 Maureen Roase, *Making melody: Puhoi 1863–2001*, Pūhoi: Roase Publications, 2001.

21 Ibid.

22 Name, date of birth, address at birth and emigrating ship of the original settlers (families of informants). The place names are in German as in 1863 with current Czech names in parentheses:

Wenzl Bayer, 21 May 1836, Chotieschau (Chotěšov) 78, *War Spirit*; Joseph Hendl (Henni), 21 May 1848, Lossin (Losina) 7, *Friedeburg*; Margaretha Hendl (née Podlesak), 6 February 1843, Mantau (Mantov) 25, *Friedeburg*; Annie Paul, 12 February 1853, Poppowa (Popov) 4, *War Spirit*; Maria Podlesak, 5 April 1840, Mantau (Mantov) 25, *War Spirit*; Johann Nepomuk Rauner, 18 July 1844, Lossin (Losina) 8, *War Spirit*; Benedict Remiger, 21 February 1851, Kostelzen (Kostelec) 53, *War Spirit*; Mary (Maria) Russek, 19 December 1850, Stich (Vstiš) 2, *War Spirit*; Paul Straka, 5 January 1830, Honositz (Honezovice) 21, *War Spirit*; Anna Wenzlick, 28 September 1836, Littitz (Litice) 10, *Liverpool*; Matthias Wech, 12 March 1863, Lossin (Losina) 34, *Liverpool*.

From Oldřich Kortus, Západočeská emigrace na Nový Zéland v 19. In *Minulostí Západočeského kraje*. Plzen: Albis International 51, (2016), pp. 227-242.

23 Email from Gerard Straka to Roger Buckton, 21 February 2023.

24 Interview with Roger Buckton, 17 August 1996.

25 Further details of Ben and Isabel Straka's lives can be found in CD format at the National Library in *Ben's Book* written by Daphne Calderwood and *Isabel's Book* written by Gerard Straka. The Pūhoi Heritage Museum can provide details of all the settlers and their families http://puhoiheritagemuseum.co.nz

Bibliography

Pūhoi music and history

Droescher, W. O. 'The Egerland-German dialect of Puhoi (North Auckland), New Zealand'. 1969. Paper archived in Auckland Public Libraries.

Goldsmith, Paul. *The rise and fall of Te Hemera Tauhia*. Auckland: Reed, 2003.

Haworth, Jennifer. 'Faith and brotherhood'. *New Zealand Geographic*, no. 21 (January–March 1994).

Heller, Wilfried with James Braund. *The 'Bohemians' in New Zealand – an ethnic group?* Auckland: Research Centre for Germanic Connections with New Zealand and the Pacific, University of Auckland, 2005.

Hurrey, Marjory. 'Down the years: a scrapbook chronicle of Puhoi: a New Zealand Bohemian settlement: 1861–1986'. 1986. Unpublished papers, Pūhoi.

King, Jean. 'Anti-German hysteria during World War I'. In *Out of the shadow of war: the German connections with New Zealand in the twentieth century*, edited by James N. Bade assisted by James Braund. Auckland: Oxford University Press, 1998, 19–24.

Kortus, Oldřich. 'Západočeská emigrace na Nový Zéland v 19'. In *Minulostí Západočeského* kraje 51, 227–42. Plzeň: Albis International, 2016.

Krippner, Christine. *Papa's Melodies*. Ōhaupō: Christine Krippner, 2003.

Mabbett, Harold. *The rock and the sky: the story of Rodney County*. Auckland: Wilson and Horton, 1977.

Mooney, Kathleen. *From the heart of Europe to the land of the Southern Cross: A story of Puhoi 1863–1963*. Pūhoi: Puhoi Centennial Publications Committee, 1963.

Roase, Maureen. *Te Grahama — Rapata Kereama: Robert Graham, 1820–1885*. Pūhoi: Roase Publications, 1998.

Roase, Maureen. *Making melody: Puhoi 1863–2001*. Pūhoi: Roase Publications, 2001.

Schmidt, Ruth. 'The settlement of Puhoi'. MA thesis, University of New Zealand, 1934.

Schwass, Margot. *All the juicy pastures: Greville Texidor and New Zealand*. Wellington: Victoria University Press, 2019.

Silk, Daniel V. *An historical narrative of the people of Puhoi, dedicated to the pioneers living and dead*. Dunedin: New Zealand Tablet Printing and Publishing Co., 1923.

Williams, Judith. 'Puhoi, the Bohemian Settlement'. In *The German connection: New Zealand and the German-speaking Europe in the nineteenth century*, edited by James N. Bade, 65–71. Auckland: Oxford University Press, 1993.

Williams, Judith. *Puhoi remembers*. Pūhoi: J. R. Williams, 1981.

Williams, Judith. 'Notebook: handwritten collection & comments on the Puhoi dialect'. (manuscript, n.d.)

Bohemian, Czech and Slovakian histories and culture

Agnew, Hugh. *The Czechs: and the lands of the Bohemian crown*. Stanford: Hoover Institution Press, 2004.

Cwach, Michael. 'Bagpipes in the Blata region of Bohemia'. Master of Music thesis, University of South Dakota, 2007.

Cwach, Michael. 'The pukl and chodsko: Aspects of linkage between a bagpipe and an ethnographic region'. PhD thesis, University of Canterbury, 2012.

Egerland-Museum. *Eghalanda halt's enk z'samm: Geschichte und Gegenwart der Egerländer Gmoin*. Marktredwitz: Egerland-Museum, 1993.

Hauptmann, Luděk. *Stod: stručné dějiny města*. Stod: Luděk Hauptmann, 1997.

Hofmann, Josef. *Deutsche Volkstrachten und Volkbräuche in West- und Südböhmen*. Karlsbad: Verlag d. Vereines, 1932.

Newmarch, Rosa. *The music of Czechoslovakia*. London: Oxford University Press, 1942.

Orr, Biddy. *A history of the Chotieschau Convent in Bohemia 1200–1946*. Matamata: Biddy Orr, 2006.

Pokorný, Jiří. *The Czech lands, 1918–1997*. Prague: Práh Press, 1994.

Salzmann, Zdenek and Vladimír Scheufler. *Komárov: A Czech farming village*. New York: Holt, Rinehart & Winston, 1974.

Sayer, Derek. *The coasts of Bohemia: A Czech history*. New Jersey: Princeton University Press, 1998.

Schreiner, Lorenz (ed.). *Eger und das Egerland: Volkskunst und brauchtum*. Munich: Langen Müller Verlag, 1988. Teich, Mikuláš (ed.). *Bohemia in history*. Cambridge: Cambridge University Press, 1998.

Song origins (bold page numbers link to the songs)

Baumann, Erich. *Deutsche Volkslieder aus Böhmen.* Nachdruck aus der 'Rittersberg-Sammlung' Ausgabe 1925 in Prag. Nürnberg: Helmut Preußler Verlag, 1984a. **48**

Baumann, Erich. Volksliedfunde bei den Egerländern in Neuseeland. In: *Der Egerländer Jg,* 35 Nr 9, S 11–13, 1984b. **50, 56**

Bauman, Erich. *Alt-Egerländer Tänze: Ein Spielbuch mit 60 Egerländer Tänzen und Liedern aus zwei Jahrhunderten.* Heidelberg: Selbstverlag des Arbeitskreises Egerländer Kulturschaffender e.V. Druck: Sulzbach-Rosenberg: Druckerei Keck, 1985. **48, 84, 90, 97**

Baumann, Erich. 'Egerländer Volkslieder aus dem ehemaligen Kreis Tachau-Pfraumberg im Egerland'. *Schriften zur Tachauer Heimatgeschichte, vol. 4.* Geretsried: Lewke Druck und Verlag, 1990. **76, 82, 84, 90, 92**

Bergmann, Alois. *Liederbuch der Egerländer.* Geislingen an der Steige: Verlag des BdEG, 1952. **40, 44, 48, 64, 86**

Blechschmidt, Manfred. 'Max August Schreyer und das Lied vom Vogelbeerbaum'. In: *Jahrbuch für Volksliedforschung* 26. Berlin: Verlag Erich Schmidt, 1981. **86**

Böhme, Franz Magnus (Hrsg). *Deutsches Kinderlied und Kinderspiel. Volksüberlieferungen aus allen Landen deutscher Zunge.* Leipzig: Breitkopf und Härtel, no. 665, 1897. **34**

Braun, Hermann. *Nordbairisches Wörterbuch des Sechsämter-, Stift- und Egerlandes.* 2 vols. Giessen: Verlag Wilhelm Schmitz, 2004. **48, 62, 64, 72**

Brosch, Albert. *Der Liederschatz des Egerlandes.* 4 vol hrsg. vom Bund der Eghalanda Gmoin e.V. Marktredwitz: Eigenverlag des BdEG, 1997. **42, 48**; no. 1457 **56, 64**; vol. 2, p. 137. **74, 82**

Buckton, Roger. *Bohemian Journey: A musical heritage in colonial New Zealand.* Wellington: Steele Roberts, 2013, pp. 18–19. **36**

Bundesliederbuch: Eine Sammlung zweistimmiger Lieder mit angedeuteter Zupfgeigenbegleitung. Hrsg. vom Bunde der Deutschen in Böhmen. Teplitz-Schönau, c. 1900. **86**

Czerny, Josef and Alois John. *Egerländer Volkslieder* Heft 2. Verein für Egerländer Volkskunde in Eger, 1901. **48**

Denz, Josef. *Die Mundart von Windisch-Eschenbach. Ein Beitrag zum Lautstand und zum Wortschatz des heutigen Nordbairischen.* Frankfurt am Main — Bern — Las Vegas: Peter Lang, 1977. **62**

Derschmidt, Hermann. *Tänze aus Oberösterreich.* 2 Bde. Linz: Landesinstitut für Volksbildung und Heimatpflege, 1985, nos 59–62. **34**

Deutsch Walter. *Das alpenländische Liederbuch.* Ravensburg: Otto Maier Verlag, 1979. **86**

Eichenseer, Adolf and Lothar E. Karrer (eds). *Freinderl, wann geh ma hoam. Wirtshauslieder aus der Oberpfalz und angrenzenden Gebieten.* Regensburg: Mittelbayerische Druck- und Verlagsgesellschaft, 3/2009, 1st edition 1999, p. 69. **28, 70, 76**

Eichenseer, Adolf and Wolfgang A. Mayer. *Volkslieder aus der Oberpfalz und angrenzenden Gebieten.* Gesungene Zwiefache. Kassel: Gustav Bosse Verlag. Reprint 2000: Regensburg: Mittelbayerischer Verlag, 1976, p. 124f. **36, 48**

Eichenseer, Adolf (ed). *Das grosse bairische Gstanzlbuch — Håt oaner oans gsunga.* München: Volk Verlag, 2014. **76**

Erk, Ludwig. *Deutscher Liederhort. Auswahl der vorzüglicheren deutschen Volkslieder, nach Wort und Weise aus der Vorzeit und Gegenwart.* vol. 2. Berlin: Breitkopf & Härtel, 1894. **30**

Euling, Karl. *Das Priamel bis Hans Rosenplüt.* Germanistische Abhandlungen 25. Hildesheim New York: Georg Olms Verlag, 1977, p. 399. **76**

Flotzinger, Rudolf. 'Augustin, Lieber'. In *Oesterreichisches Musiklexikon* online. **74**

Gleichmann, Elise (ed). *Altvöterischa Schlumperliedla und Verschla aus Oberfranken.* o.O.: o.J. Nachdruck der Ausgabe Lichtenfels: H. O. Schulze, [1933], c. 2000, S 69 [2]. **90, 92**

Haffner, Gerhard. *Unsere schönsten Volkslieder.* München und Zürich: Delphin Verlag GmbH, 1979 **90**

Harwalik, Hans (ed.). *Lieder von daheim.* Freyung: Heimatsammlung Stadt Winterberg, 1993. **42**

Heil, Josef. *Egerländer Tanzfibel.* Geislingen an der Steige: Egerland-Verlag, 1963. **48**

Heimrath, Ralf. 'Bayerisch Duarl' und 'Unser alte Kath'. In: *Sänger- und Musikantenzeitung. Zweimonatsschrift für Volksmusik* Jg. 45 Heft 4 S, 2002, pp. 299–303. **48**

Heimrath, Ralf. 'Puhoi — The Agony of a German Language Island in New Zealand'. In Heimrath, Ralf and Arndt Kremer (eds). *Insularity. Small Worlds in Linguistic and Cultural Perspectives.* Würzburg: Königshausen & Neumann, 2015, p. 69. **84**

Heimrath, Ralf. 'Das Lied vom Vogelbeerbaum in

Neuseeland?' In *Der Egerländer*. Stammeszeitschrift — Eghalanda Bundeszeiting Jg. 72/5. Nürnberg: Preußler Verlag S 2–4, 2020. **86**

Hofmann, Josef. *28 Egerländer Volkslieder*. Karlsbad: Selbstverlag, 1901. **40, 42**

Hruschka, Alois and Wendelin Toischer. 'Deutsche Volkslieder aus Böhmen', hrsg. V. Deutschen Verein zur Verbreitung gemeinnütziger Kenntnisse, Prag: Selbstverlag des Vereins, Kommission bei Cnobloch in Leipzig, 1891, p. 346. **40, 42, 50, 64**; p. 353. **84**

Jindrich, J. (Chodská 1926–30) in *Národ v písni*, Praha: L. Mazáč, p. **56, 30**

John, Alois and Josef Czerny. *Egerländer Volkslieder* 2. Eger: Verein für Egerländer Volkskunde, 1901. **40, 42**

Jungbauer, Gustav. *Bibliographie des Deutschen Volksliedes in Böhmen*. Beiträge zur deutsch-böhmischen Volkskunde Bd. 8. Prag: Verlag: J. G. Calv'sche k.u.k. Hof- u. Universitäts-Buchhandlung, 1913, no. 2140. **84**

Jungbauer, Gustav and Herbert Horntrich. *Volkslieder der Sudetendeutschen*. Kassel Bärenreiter-Verlag, 1938, p. 652. **82**

Kellermann, Michael. Wer mir und meiner Schwarzn wås tuat. https://www.stammtischmusik.at/noten/wermirundmeiner.htm [accessed 26.06.2016]. **48**

Kiss, Elly. *Deutsche Volkstanzüberlieferunge n im südlichen Transdanubien*. In Beiträge zur Volkskunde der Ungarndeutschen. Bd. 2, S. 1979, pp. 185–228. **34**

Kobell, Franz v. 'Oberbayerische Lieder mit ihren Singweisen'. In *Auftrage und mit Unterstützung Seiner Majestät des Königs für das bayerische Gebirgsvolk*. Mit Bildern von A. v. Ramberg. 2. Auflage. München: Holzschnitt und Verlag von Braun & Schneider, 1871. **86**

Köferl, Josef. 'Supplement zur Heimatkunde des politischen Bezirks Tachau'. In *Köferl-Werk*. Geretsried: Verlag Lewke, 1895 (reprint 1985), p. 330. **82**

Kreger, Helmut. 'Brouder liaderle saan mir baranand'. *Tirschenreuther Liedermappe* Part 2. Regensburg: Oberpfälzer Volksmusikfreunde e.V., 2002. **30**

Kremser, Eduard. *Wiener Lieder und Tänze* vol. 1. Vienna: Buch- und Kunstverlag Gerlach & Wiedling, 1912. **86**

Kunz, T. A. *Böhmische Nationalgesaenge und Taenze*. Praha: Ústav pro etnografii a folkloristiku AV ČR [Institute for ethnography and folkloristics Czech Republic], vol. 1, Facsimile vol. 2, transcription and translation. [1825] **48**

Männer, Karl. *Tänze aus der Oberpfalz*. Regensburg: Oberpfälzer Volksmusikfreunde, 1971. **90**

Meier, Ernst. *Schwäbische Volkslieder mit ausgewählten Melodien*. Aus mündlicher Überlieferung gesammelt. Berlin: DeGruyter, 1855, p. 20, no. 4. **30**

Menzl, Josef. 'Wer mir und meiner Schwarzen'. In Menzl, Josef, *Wer nicht singt, der stinkt*. Textheft zur gleichnamigen CD, 2018. https://kapelle-josefmenzl.de/images/downloads/Textheft.pdf [accessed 08.04/2024]. **48**

Nagel, Georg, 2016. https://www.lieder-archiv.de/o_du_lieber_augustin-notenblatt_100091.html [accessed 20/02/2020].

Novák, Vítězlav. *Národ v písni*. Prague: L. Mazáč, 1940, p. 56. **30**

Obermair, Gilbert. *Lieder der unvergessenen Heimat*. Volks- und Heimatlieder aus Mittle- und Ostdeutschland. München: Wilhelm Heyne Verlag, 1981.

Piger, Franz Paul. 'Das Schaderhuptel in der Iglauer Sprachinsel'. In *Zeitschrift für österreichische Volkskunde* Jg. IV. Vienna und Prague: Verlag F. Temsky, 1898, pp. 6–28. **82**

Pimmer, Karl Josef. *Volkslieder und Volksmusik aus dem Böhmerwald*. Abensberg: Selbstverlag, 1976. **42, 64**

Queri, Georg. *Kraftbayrisch. Ein Wörterbuch der erotischen und skatologischen Redensarten der Altbayern. Mit Belegen aus dem Volkslied, der bäuerlichen Erzählung und dem Volkswitz*. München: Verlag Piper & Co., 1912. **28, 42**

Schmeller, Johann Andreas. *Bayerisches Wörterbuch*. Sonderausgabe der von G. Karl Frommann bearbeiteten. 2nd edition. 4 vol. München: R. Oldenbourg Verlag, vols. 1–4. **42, 48, 62**

Schötz, Franz and Hans Wax. *Singen im Tirschenreuther Land. Lieder aus dem Stiftland, Steinwald und der Kemnather Region*. Kallmünz: Verlag Laßleben, 2006. **86**

Spack, Alexander (ed.), *Volkslieder und Kinderreime aus den Wolgakolonien*. Russlanddeutsche Literatursammlung Ausgabe 3. Neudruck der Ausgabe von, 1914. Die Geschichte der Wolgadeutschen, 2010. https://wolgadeutsche.net [accessed 02.05.2021]. **74**

Spurný, Tomáš. *Nordböhmische Volkslieder aus der Sammlung von Adolf König. Notenaufzeichnungen und Dokumente eines Reichenberger Volksliedsammlers aus den Jahren 1904–1934*. Passau: Lehrstuhl für Volkskunde an der Universität Passau, 2000. **90**

Sykora, Josef and Michl Reiter. *Singendes Egerland. Ein- und zweistimmige Egerländer Lieder*. Nürnberg: Egerland-Verlag Helmut Preußler, 1976, p. 72f. **40, 42, 48, 64, 86**

Tirschenreuther Liedermappe vol. 4. Lieder aus dem Stiftland, Steinwald und Kemnather Land. Regensburg: Oberpfälzer Volksmusikfreunde e.V., 1996 (2nd ed. 2002). **84**

Tyllner, Lubomír (ed.) in collaboration with Ralf Heimrath, Wolfgang Mayer and Eliška Čáňová. *T. A. Kunz. Böhmische Nationalgesaenge und Taenze*. [České národní zpěvy a tance]. Prague: Ústav pro etnografii a folkloristiku AV ČR, vol. 1, facsimile vol. 2, transcription and translation, 1995. **48**

Urban, Michael. 'As da Heimat'. *Eine Sammlung deutscher Volkslieder aus dem ostfränkischen Sprachgebiet der österreichischen Provinz Böhmen als Beitrag zur Culturgeschichte Deutschböhmens*. Plan: Druck von Schwaab & Müller, 1894, p. 103. **42, 50**

Webinger, Alfred. 'Deutsche Bauernliebe. Beiträge zur Erforschung der Minne im Leben und Liede, vorzüglich der oberösterreichischen und steirischen Bauernschaft. Mit 276 Volksweisen'. In Krauss, Friedrich S. (ed.): *Das Minnelied des deutschen Land- und Stadtvolkes* vol. 2, *Abhandlungen und Sammlungen*. Leipzig: Ethnologischer Verlag Dr Friedrich S. Krauss, 1929. **42**

Weckerlin, Jean-Baptiste (ed.). *Chansons populaires de l' Alsace vol. 2*. Paris: Maisonneuve et Cie, 1883, p. **82**

Williams, Judith R. *Puhoi remembers. 1863–1981 Church, school and social life in a Bohemian Village*. Warkworth: Rodney & Waitemata Times Ltd, 1981. **97**

Zehetner, Ludwig. *Bairisches Deutsch. Lexikon der deutschen Sprache in Altbayern*. (2nd edition). München: Hugendubel Verlag, 1998. **62**

Ziemann, Johanna. 'Heißa Kathreinerle, schnür' dir die Schuh". https://www.liederlexikon.de/lieder/heissa_kathereinerle_ich_schnuer_dir_die_schuh [accessed 18.03.2022]. **82**

Websites

https://www.lieder-archiv.de/jeder_eseltreiber-notenblatt_402264.html **28**

http://www.sulinet.hu/oroksegtar/data/magyarorszagi_nemzetisegek/nemetek/beitrage_zur_volkskunde_der_ungarndeutschen/1979/pages/008_deutsche_volkstanzuberlieferungen.html **34**

https://www.stammtischmusik.at/noten/wermirundmeiner.htm [19.04.2018] **48**

http://docplayer.org/22001225-Wer-nicht-singt-der-stinkt-liedtexte-zum-kraeftig-mitsingen.html **48**

https://www.volksliederarchiv.de/vergebliche-liebesmueh/ [22.01.2020] **72**

http://www.meck-pomm-hits.de/land-leute/traditionen/kinderlieder-mecklenburg-vorpommern-norddeutschland/ **72**

https://www.musiklexikon.ac.at/ml/musik_A/Augustin_lieber.xml **74**

https://wolgadeutsche.net/bibliothek/books/Ausgabe3.pdf **74**

https://www.lieder-archiv.de/o_du_lieber_augustin-notenblatt_100091.html **74**

http://www.puhoidialect.net.nz/ogg/atbs%20saying%20if%20my%20mother%20hadn't%20sewed%2011%20benstraka.ogg [06.05.2021] **76**

http://www.puhoidialect.net.nz/ogg/atfr%20saying%20if%20my%20mother%20hadn't%20sewed%20fredrauner.ogg [06.05.2021] **76**

http://www.puhoidialect.net.nz/ogg/atbs%20saying%20drinking%20song%2011%20benstraka.ogg **78**

http://www.liederlexikon.de/lieder/heissa_kathreinerle_ich_schnuer_dir_die_schuh **82**

https://ingeb.org/Lieder/mirsanja.html **86**

https://www.dancilla.com/wiki/index.php/Siebenschritt **90**

https://www.dancilla.com/wiki/index.php/Eins,_zwei,_drei,_vier,_fünf,_sechs,_sieben **90**

http://www.deutsche-lieder-online.de/volkslied-und-kinderlied-1-2-3-wo-ist-denn-mein-schatz-geblieben.html **90**

https://www.dancilla.com/wiki/index.php/Siebenschritt **90**

https://www.volksliederarchiv.de/bruederchen-komm-tanz-mit-mir/ **90**

https://www.dancilla.com/wiki/index.php?title=Volkst%C3%A4nze_getanzt_in_Oberfranken **97**

https://www.zachmeier.de/sua-tanzn-mia-volkstaenze-aus-der-oberpfalz.html **97**

https://www.bairisch-landlerisch.de/spitzbuam-polka/ **97**

https://www.youtube.com/watch?v=VX7e6_3jzqc) (Lithuania) **97**

https: www.kickery.com.polka **97**

Explanatory notes

The popular and traditional instrument of Pūhoi is the button accordion. Players normally read all tunes in the key of C. Hence, all the tunes in Becher's manuscript book are in the key of C. In keeping with this tradition, we have favoured the key of C in this collection. However, having in mind the need to encourage singing, other keys have been chosen for some of the songs so that the range of each song suits the average human voice.

The old button accordions played only two or three chords — the primary chords. In keeping with this practice, only primary chords have been used, without additional 7ths. It is expected that musicians will modify these chords according to their own tastes.

The cover of the cassette recording *Accordians of Puhoi* showing Fred and Laurie Rauner with button accordions and Joe Tolhopf with the piano accordion. *Recorder Centre, 1996*

In compiling this collection, there has been an effort to achieve a balance between an archival record of Pūhoi songs and the need to provide a repertoire that is singable for a range of singing groups. For a majority of the songs, the whole text and tune have been recorded from Pūhoi sources and are offered as such. But there are some songs in which only a fragment has been recalled.

For example, in *I u ma(n ålts Wei,* only the first eight bars were recorded by Droescher. The German folk song *Heißa Kathreinerle* has those same eight bars but also two more sets of eight bars, which gives the song a sense of completeness and makes it a delight to sing. The appendix (see page 146) provides explanations of the various sources for each song.

The songs reproduced here are the texts and music discovered in our research. There is still much music that has not been included. For example, many tunes are to be found in the Becher manuscript book and these and others were played by the Puhoi Band on their 1993 and 1996 recordings but the compilers could not find any song text in New Zealand or Egerland sources. For this collection, Czech song sources were not searched.

Many tunes in the Becher manuscript book cannot be traced back to Egerlander sources. Some are known to be English tunes and there are those that may have been composed in Pūhoi by musicians such as Charles Becher. Joe Tolhopf also wrote some fine songs and tunes.

Acknowledgements

These Bohemian songs are a reflection of family and community. Similarly, this presentation of the songs has been a family and community affair: families and friends of the compilers and the wider Pūhoi community, including those who live beyond Pūhoi.

Hours of voluntary work have gone into reading and reviewing the drafts and finding pictures and other source material. The compilers gratefully acknowledge you all. The following are some of the friends who have helped in these ways:

Lenka Absolonová, Adrian Anderson, Gabrielle Aumont, Carol, Emma and Andrew Buckton, Karen Camp and the Ōhaupō community, Michael Cwach, Judith Geare (Goethe Society, Wellington), Wendy Hayton, Margret Heimrath, Christine Krippner, Petr Nováček, Irena Novotná, Dame Claudia Orange, Kate Shevland, Jenny Schollum (Pūhoi Heritage Museum), Stephen Schollum, Roger Steele, Gerard Straka, Lukáš Svoboda, Sheryll Titford, Claire Weyland, staff from the Auckland University library archives and the Cheb Museum, Czech Republic, and German Embassy in Wellington.

To all those descendants and others noted in these pages who so willingly and patiently gave their time, showing their devotion to the old culture, we also give our hearty thanks. Without your dedication, the documentation and preservation of the Puhoian dialect songs would have been impossible.

Finally, we acknowledge the kind and thoughtful people who pledged to buy a book and give one to the Pūhoi Heritage Museum. Your pledges made the publication possible.

In 1765 the revered German writer Johann Wolfgang Goethe went as a young man from Frankfurt am Main to study in Leipzig in eastern Germany. At first, he hardly understood the people there and wrote in his diary: 'Jede Provinz liebt ihren Dialekt, denn er ist doch eigentlich das Element, in welchem die Seele ihren Atem schöpft.' (Each province loves its dialect, because this is actually the element, in which the soul draws its breath.)

When the first settlers of Pūhoi came from Europe during the years 1863 to 1876, they brought their dialect and their songs as 'the breath of their souls' to their new home. Their descendants sustained this language for over a century as an important expression of their German-Bohemian identity.

About the editors

Judith Williams lived her early years in the village of Waiwera and started her schooling at the Pūhoi convent school. She formed friendships with local Bohemian families and these early relationships fostered her interest in the local dialect, its songs and dances. She trained as a teacher and studied German to Master's level at the University of Auckland, followed by three years teaching English at secondary level in Oldenburg, Germany.

Williams was intensely proud of being a descendant of the early settlers in the area (Pittner) and her decision to learn German and to live in Germany derived from her early links with Pūhoi families. So it was unsurprising that later she returned to Pūhoi, and developed a smallholding there with sheep and chickens.

At this time, Williams began a second career, in journalism. She helped establish the Puhoi Historical Society in 1976 and contributed to many community activities. In 2014 she was awarded the Queen's Service Medal for services to the community. She continued to visit Germany and the Czech Republic and fostered strong links with Egerlander visitors to Pūhoi.

At that time the old songs and dances were a regular part of local events, and traditional musical instruments were often played at the local pub. Williams's role in documenting these traditions cannot be overestimated. She was a well-known identity for many years, taking great interest in traditional cultural activities and doing all she could to ensure that they blossomed and thrived.

Dr Ralf Heimrath majored in German language, literature and history at the Ludwig Maximilian University of Munich. His distinguished scholarly career encompasses teaching and leadership positions at a Bavarian open-air museum, the National University of Mongolia and the University of Malta. His research interests include German dialectology, contact linguistics and the history of folk music. He is the author and editor of a wealth of publications, including a number of folk-song collections. As well as his scholarly expertise, his family heritage made him an asset to this project. His mother and grandparents, as well as the parents of his wife Margret, came from the same region in Egerland as the Pūhoi settlers. Brought up speaking the same dialect, they knew many of the songs and tunes, especially as his grandparents loved making this genre of music. Later Heimrath lived in the Upper Palatinate in Bavaria, which adjoins the region of the Egerland and has an almost identical dialect.

As one of the few scholarly experts in the dialect, he has served his culture by working with several cultural organisations: from 2007 to 2009 he was the president of the Bund der Egerländer Gmoin (Union of the Egerland Communities) and in 2015 he was awarded the Egerländer Kulturpreis Johannes-von-Tepl, the highest award given by any Egerlander association.

Dr Roger Buckton and his family moved to Pūhoi in 1990 and discovered the rich world of Bohemian music Kiwi style. His professional music career and interest in early European music helped him appreciate that in his neighbourhood there was a wealth of European music which had been undergoing a transformation since the arrival of the early settlers in 1863. He quickly went about recording this music, and two cassettes (later CDs) and a documentary film for the University of Auckland were produced from 1993 to 1996.

After years of research and performances of the music, Buckton's book *Bohemian Journey: A Musical Heritage in Colonial New Zealand* was published in time for Pūhoi's 150th anniversary in 2013. The simultaneous publication of Judith Williams's book *It Takes a Whole Village: the People of Puhoi* showed Buckton the cultural value of her collection of song and verse texts and was the catalyst for matching song texts and music to realise the rich heritage of song which was fast disappearing with the loss of the language.

Buckton was an Adjunct Associate-Professor at the University of Canterbury and lectured in ethno-music, musicianship and music education. He continues to perform on the dudelsack, alongside other instruments of early music. His aim is to promote the songs and music in this collection so that these unique Kiwi-Bohemian musical gems take their place in the multicultural heritage of Aotearoa New Zealand.

A scene from a village inn in German-speaking Heiligenkreuz (Czech: Újezd Svatého Kříže), Bohemia in 1863, painted by Quido Mánes. Hanging on the wall (top left) is a dudelsack of similar type to the original Pūhoi instrument brought out with the early settlers (Heiligenkreuz was just 38 kilometres from Poppowa, where some of the Pūhoi settlers came from, including dudelsack player Joseph Paul. Heiligenkreuz was a German-speaking village just beyond the Egerland ethnographic area, so there are no examples of the Chotieschau tracht such as the Mützl (velvet cap) noted in the song, *Der wos döi bayrisch Duadl will hom*. Although difficult to see, there is a JM monogram on the bag to the right. Quido Mánes has depicted his brother, the Czech artist Josef Mánes (in a top hat and holding a pipe) as a dozing tourist among the villagers. And what are the villagers discussing? Perhaps they are wondering about the fate of their friends from around Chotieschau and Mies who went to that faraway country of New Zealand. *Vesnická hospoda, 1863 (A village inn, 1863), Quido Mánes, by permission of Prague Castle, Treasury of Art*

Index

Page numbers in bold indicate images.

All known sources of photos have been acknowledged. Please note that those credited as PHS are from the Puhoi Heritage Museum. Please notify Roger Buckton if any unknown source can be named. These songs, rhymes and music and associated information represent the work of many years of collecting and editing. Please notify Roger Buckton of any discrepancies, additional material and sources: roger.buckton@icloud.com

Published with the support of the German Embassy in New Zealand

MASSEY UNIVERSITY PRESS

First published in 2025 by Massey University Press
Private Bag 102904, North Shore Mail Centre
Auckland 0745, New Zealand
www.masseypress.ac.nz

Front cover photograph: Detail of dancers at the 2016 celebrations in Pūhoi of the arrival of the ship *Liverpool* into Auckland in March 1866, bringing 31 Bohemian settlers (see page 2–3 for full image). *Christine Krippner*
Back cover photographs: (Above) Singing at the Pūhoi pub, c. 1970. *PHS 0071*; (Below) Philip Wech on dudelsack and Simon Bayer on accordion, Pūhoi, 1966. *PHS 1403*
Part openers: The Bohemian Dance Group posed for the North Shore Photography Club in the early 2000s and some of these images are used for the part openers. Page 10: Jenny Schollum (left) and Kathryn Mankelow; Page 98: Kathryn Mankelow, with Jenny Schollum at right; Page 144: Jenny Schollum, with Vanessa Monks and Lawrence Schischka on the far side of the circle.

Design by Kate Barraclough

A catalogue record for this book is available from the National Library of New Zealand

Printed and bound in China by Everbest Printing Investment Limited

ISBN: 978-1-99130-903-7